Praise

'This is a simple but pragmatic step-by-step guide for a line manager to support the development of their team members.'
— **Ann Pickering**, Chartered Companion, CIPD

'The impetus and imperative behind the book is excellent – these are much needed conversations, especially in today's turbulent, difficult world of employment when employees face so many new and unplanned for challenges. Antoinette's wisdom, authority and empathy are very clear.'
— **Mike Elliston**, Writer and Visiting Fellow, Hatfield College, Durham University

'As a global career development influencer and seasoned corporate facilitator, it was a pleasure to read this impactful book. *Confident Career Conversations* will be a game-changer in the world of work and a must read for Senior Management, HR, managers and employees. The book is written in a conversational and friendly manner with pragmatic, futuristic and evidence-based content to increase employee employability and enjoyability. The manager questions are thought provoking, intriguing and lead to a mutually beneficial dialogue. The career conversation model and toolkit are needed in the current fragile times.'
— **Raza Abbas**, Global Career Development Influencer, Seasoned Corporate Facilitator, Coach

'As someone that has not had what you might define as a traditional career, I found this book resonated deeply with me both as a person and also as someone that has built or been part of building a number of teams across a range of sectors. During a time when finding and retaining talent is a difficult and costly enterprise, this book marries sound theories with practical actions, all underpinned by something I wholeheartedly agree with, the need to have a conversation with people. Don't assume, don't imagine; ask and engage in an active ongoing dialogue and you have a much better chance of aligning your aims with their plans and desires. A great practical read.'

— **Martin Spiller**, Senior Lecturer at Cranfield School of Management, Entrepreneur and Serial NED

Confident
Career
Conversations

Empower your employees
for career growth
and retention

Antoinette Oglethorpe

Rethink

First published in Great Britain in 2023 by Rethink Press (www.rethinkpress.com)

This book is dedicated to the memory of my late parents who believed in me, inspired me and empowered me to realise my potential and fulfil my ambitions.

Contents

Foreword

A couple of decades ago, I helped a large employer in the transport industry investigate causes of employee turnover. One issue that emerged was people felt discouraged from discussing career moves with their immediate supervisor or anyone in their team. They were afraid that they would be seen as disloyal, and as a result would miss bonuses and be given all the rubbish jobs. They were even reluctant to talk about their career ambitions with other managers in case word got back – so they looked for their career opportunities outside the company. It didn't help that line managers were generally inept at envisioning career paths different from their own. The only people employees felt safe opening up to were mentors, who would provide confidentiality and a broader perspective on opportunities. Making mentoring much more widely available was one of the solutions to this company's retention problems.

Contrast this with the soft drinks company Smoothie, where employees are hired with the expectation of open conversations about when they will take the learning that they have gained working from the company and apply it elsewhere, often in creating their own businesses. Or with the concept of the talent factory, which I first described in the 1970s. As a journalist at that time, I was intrigued why some companies were a breeding ground for a disproportionate number of the most senior people across industry in areas such as marketing, human resources and finance. In each case, they hired bright young people, gave them extraordinary responsibilities, along with the support to rise to the challenge, and had frequent developmental conversations with them about longer-term career ambitions. It created a 'jet engine' effect – whenever someone moved on to greater things, a host of others were queuing up to take their place.

In my research into talent management, I identified a number of key conversations relating to successful partnerships between organisations and career-minded employees. The first was the conversation an employee has with themselves: what do they really want from their life and career, what are their developed, emerging and embryonic strengths, what do they need to do to ensure opportunities come to them? The second conversation was between the employee and either or both their boss and a mentor. Where and how can they find opportunities to develop new skills and knowledge, to expand their networks and build reputation and track record? A third was the broader conversations that happened (far too infrequently) between top management, human resources and employees around how the organisation/employee partnership might evolve.

Underpinning all these factors is the creation within teams and within organisations of an environment where career ambitions can be shared openly and supported. It requires a major mind-shift in how organisations think about jobs, in a future where long-term tenure in a single employer or role is less and less likely. In this new climate:

- No-one 'owns' a job role – it is leased to them in a social exchange that focuses on performance (for the company) and learning (for the employee)

- The question 'Am I the right person for this role as it evolves?' is one that employees ideally ask before the company does. It's followed by 'Where can I best use my talents and energy?'

- Creating new job roles is a shared responsibility for both employees and employers

- Career conversations happen continuously and openly

- Everyone in a team takes responsibility for both their own performance, learning and well-being and that of their team colleagues

In this book, Antoinette provides both the background to effective career conversations and practical guidance on how to do them well. She offers a simple but pragmatic framework that anyone who oversees other employees can apply if they take their role as people developer seriously. At root, this is a matter of legacy. People rarely remember the boss who delivered results. They remember the bosses who enabled them to grow.

— **David Clutterbuck**, Founder of Clutterbuck CMI and Author

Introduction

When we're faced with challenges and stress from all directions, and worst of all, fear of speaking out, managers and employees can find it hard to talk about career development. We know that people are the key to business growth and success. Research tells us that engaging with and empowering employees boosts performance by 15-30%.[1] Organisations want to maximise performance and employees want to maximise their careers. These goals are not one and the same. The key to keeping and growing your best people is to help them develop their careers in line with the needs of the business. That relies on open, honest and effective conversations.

---

[1] Gallup, 'The Powerful Relationship Between Employee Engagement and Team Performance' (Gallup, 2020), www.gallup.com/workplace/321032/employee-engagement-meta-analysis-brief.aspx, accessed 22 March 2023

Talented employees want to know where they stand in the organisation now and what their possibilities for the future are. They want direction on what and where they need to develop and they will seek feedback and support in their efforts. If they can have honest and open two-way conversations with managers and mentors, they will feel more engaged in their work and more committed to the organisation.

With the cost of hiring and retaining top talent becoming increasingly expensive and competitive, this is more important than ever. Employees have, and want, more choice over their careers. There are high risks to organisations who don't support their employees, but opening up a sensitive issue like career progression can weigh heavily on even the most experienced shoulders. The big question is, 'How can I have engaging career conversations that empower employees to take ownership of their own development while providing them with the information and support they need?'

If you manage, supervise or mentor anyone, you can expect that, at some stage, they will ask you how they can progress in your organisation. The term 'people managers' is used throughout the book to include all people who become these 'go-to' people in their organisations. This book was designed with you all in mind. It prepares you for the conversations that will help your employees feel satisfied in their roles no matter what their career ambitions are.

Whatever role you have in your organisation, the practical resources in *Confident Career Conversations* provide you with the fundamental answers to the following:

- What does a great career conversation look like?

- What are its main components and structure?

- How long is it supposed to be?

- What questions should be asked?

- How can I help employees take ownership of their career development?

- How can I support people who have been in their roles a long time?

- How can I develop employees who are happy in their roles or don't know what they want?

- What can I do if the organisation can't accommodate what employees want?

- How can I create the company culture required for success?

My Career Conversations Model offers the necessary structure and tools you'll need to have those meaningful career conversations in only twenty minutes. No complex process and little or no paperwork. You'll be able to:

- Help employees feel more satisfied in their current role no matter what their ambitions.

- Encourage employees to identify development opportunities and take steps that will help them and the organisation.

- Have conversations that make employees want to stay with the organisation rather than go elsewhere.

- Have a flexible approach, which means employees take ownership for their career development and don't look to you for all the answers.

Over my thirty-year career, I have developed managers and employees for a wide range of organisations from Prudential and Saint-Gobain to the United Nations Development Programme (UNDP) and UNESCO.

My interest in career management stemmed from a personal experience. You may be surprised to hear that I consider myself fortunate that I was made redundant from my first proper job. It was voluntary redundancy from P&G, an excellent company. This was where my passion for leadership development and career management first started and I've never looked back. Most importantly, because they're an excellent company, my redundancy package included outplacement support in the form of a career coach. Bear in mind that I wasn't the mature, measured individual I am today. At the ripe old age of twenty-seven, the kindest way to describe myself was confident and self-assured. (The more accurate description was probably cocky and arrogant.) The economy was very different in the nineties and I'd had it easy. I'd got a good degree from university and I'd had my pick of graduate jobs with blue chip companies. I accepted a job in product research with P&G. Four and a half years later, when I decided I was more interested in people than washing powders, I fully expected to just be able to do what I wanted.

Thank goodness I had my career coach to save me from my naivety. He explained to me, 'You care about your career. Organisations care about their businesses. You've got to connect what you want to do with what the organisation wants, to be able to develop the career that you want.' Four months later, I started my new job as a Training Manager and I never looked back. The thing that saddened me is that employees only get support with their careers to help them leave a company rather than to help them stay. Since then, I've been even more passionate about helping organisations make the connection between how they develop their employees and how employees develop their careers. It's a win-win for everyone. That's the primary focus of this book.

Confident Career Conversations will provide you with the essential tools to make those conversations easy and to identify how you can best empower your employees' career development. I will also help you discover ideas and strategies to deal with specific career conversation challenges so that you:

- Retain your employees
- Lessen your recruitment challenge
- Improve the employee experience

The book is divided into four sections:

- Part 1: The importance of career conversations and how to set the scene for them to be successful.

- Part 2: The characteristics of effective career conversations, plus an introduction to the Career Conversation Model and Toolkit.

- Part 3: An in-depth look at those tools, along with practical understanding of how to use them in career conversations, keeping it as simple as possible.

- Part 4: Career conversations in practice, including some challenges or concerns you might have previously experienced.

Throughout the book, I will share not only my experience of working with clients, but also that of my team (fondly known as Team AO).

Books, particularly, allow us to learn from anywhere in our own time and at our own pace. To make that work for you while reading this book, use your workplace challenges as a basis for learning. Your learning will not take place in the hours you spend digesting the content. It will happen when you put the ideas into practice. You may want to reflect on your experience by discussing with your peers, your coaches, your managers and your mentors so you get that rich experience.

Confident Career Conversations is not simply ideas and theories. I have written it to inspire managers, mentors and HR professionals with practical tools and techniques that are proven to deliver results. Those tools and techniques are grounded in experience. I have used them to manage not just my own career, but also to support hundreds of others to develop professionally. Developing great employees relies on connecting their career ambitions with the goals of your organisation. In that way, you build a chain reaction of engaged, empowered people creating a better future for themselves, their colleagues, their clients and their communities. This book will give you the skills and confidence to have the career conversations you need.

PART 1
LET'S TALK CAREERS

Your company's culture is not what is written on the website. It's what employees live and experience every day. It is not about laying out a yellow brick road for employees to follow. It is about providing them with challenge and growth as part of their working life.

In his best-selling book *Drive: The Surprising Truth About What Motivates Us*,[2] Daniel Pink highlights research into motivation. He states that our core motivators are purpose, mastery and autonomy. In situations where people are paid fairly, this trio drives, engages and stimulates them to do their best work.

---

[2] D Pink, *Drive: The Surprising Truth About What Motivates Us* (Canongate Books Ltd, 13 January 2011)

In this section, we'll discuss the importance of career conversations and how to set the scene for them to be successful. We'll look at the new rules of career growth in an ever-changing workplace and who is responsible for career management in the workplace. We'll look at the implications of when career management isn't looked after as well as the benefits of when it is.

1
The New Rules
Of Career Growth

7 0% of employees are dissatisfied with future career opportunities at their organisation. That's the conclusion of the Corporate Executive Board (CEB) in their paper, 'The New Path Forward'.[3] They describe a chasm between what employees are looking for from their careers and the support they are getting from managers. CEB's research says that, 'Lack of career opportunities or lack of perceived career opportunities is the primary driver of attrition even above compensation and people management.' In other words, the adage that employees leave organisations because of their managers no longer seems to be the case. Now,

---

3   G Khoza, 'The New Path Forward: Creating Compelling Careers for Employees and Organizations' (CEB Corporate Leadership Council, 2016), www.academia.edu/29816487/The_New_Path_Forward_Creating_Compelling_Careers_for_Employees_and_Organizations, accessed 23 March 2023

they leave because of their careers. That shouldn't be a surprise. A paper based on research by Gallup[4] states,

> 'People are looking for more than just a paycheck. They want purpose and meaning from their work. They want to be known for what makes them unique. And they want relationships, particularly with a manager who can coach them to the next level.'

While employees are dissatisfied with career opportunities, organisations are concerned about skills shortages. CEB's research also shows that three-quarters of HR professionals worry they won't have the internal capabilities they need in the next three to five years. This will hinder organisations' abilities to innovate, grow and execute their business strategies.

A lot of employee disengagement has to do with a disconnect between expectations and reality. Every company I know promotes itself as offering 'great career progression'. This may help them to hire rock stars, but if the experience of those rock stars is a lack of growth, keeping them proves to be difficult.

According to the Gallup World Poll, based on an average working period of forty-one years, this equates to 81,396

---

4   Gallup, 'Building a High-Development Culture Through Your Employee Engagement Strategy' (Gallup, 21 February 2020), www.gallup.com/workplace/285800/development-culture-engagement-paper-2019.aspx, accessed 23 March 2023

hours in an average person's lifetime.[5] In fact, some of us may even work seventy- or eighty-hour weeks depending on the culture of our industries or specific workplaces. This estimate is conservative. Another estimate by Gallup using different factors calculated that people work over 115,000 hours in a lifetime. Whatever the right calculation, it is way too long to be unhappy. Achieving purpose, mastery and autonomy through our work is critical if we are going to stay motivated.

1. Purpose (ie, this is important to me): People who find purpose in their work are the most motivated. Purpose is what gets them out of bed in the morning and into work without groaning and grumbling. It's something that they can't fake.

2. Mastery (ie, I want to get better at this): Mastery describes our natural wish to get better at doing tasks. It's why learning a language or an instrument can be so frustrating at first. If you feel like you're not getting anywhere, your interest flags and you may even give up. A sense of progress, not just in our work but in our abilities, contributes to our inner drive.

3. Autonomy (ie, it's my idea): Autonomy reflects our natural inclination for self-direction. We're all built with inner drive, so we don't want someone else telling us what to do unless we ask them.

---

5   Gallup, 'State of the Global Workplace: 2022 Report' (Gallup, 2022), www.gallup.com/workplace/349484/state-of-the-global-workplace-2022-report.aspx, accessed 23 March 2023

The traditional world of work

Jobs and careers have gone through a few big shifts if you go back far enough. In the 19th century, most people worked in agriculture. Later, in the industrial era, urbanisation and rapid technological change created factories. Lots of people worked on assembly lines. Then, the post-World War 2 economic boom created the middle class, suburbs and bureaucracy. Corporations were born. The industrial assembly line inclined upward into the corporate ladder and the word 'career' entered the common lexicon. Career used to mean a life-long relationship with a company. You gave 30 to 40 years' service, you climbed a corporate ladder and you reached the top by getting promoted incrementally. Then, you retired with a gold watch and a pension.

I asked this question in a webinar for a client recently: 'If you had to create an image to represent career progression, what would it be?' I received the following answers:

- Steps to climb.

- A linear, incremental graph.

- A ladder.

- A road.

- A staircase.

- A climbing tree.

These are all traditional answers. In the 21st century, do we really all progress by climbing steadily upwards? They surprised me, and here's why.

The world of work is changing

The world is different now. We are in a state of constant change. These days, there is no such thing as a 'job for life'. Whole industries have been created in the last few decades alone, with many likely to disappear in the coming years. At the same time, attitudes to work are changing. Younger generations increasingly reject the predictability and stability of the traditional career path. Instead, they want a more varied, interesting and flexible one. As we think about and plan for the future of work, there are five key shifts we need to be aware of:

1. **Technology:** Exponential advances in technology are changing the world around us every day. Artificial intelligence, big data, robotics and automation aim to reduce labour and help with complex tasks. These same innovations bring uncertainty and worry for those whose lives and jobs may be affected by these changes. Estimates show 45% of the jobs people perform today could be automated using future technological reforms.[6] With these losses come

---

6   McKinsey & Company, 'Jobs Lost, Jobs Gained: Workforce Transitions in A Time of Automation' (McKinsey Global Institute, December 2017), www.mckinsey.com/~/media/BAB489A30B724BECB5DEDC41E9BB9FAC.ashx, accessed 23 March 2023

new opportunities, at least for those flexible enough to adapt. We've seen through successive human revolutions – agricultural, industrial, digital – how new technology inevitably brings in new jobs.

2. **Changing demographics:** The makeup of the global population is changing, with significant and direct impacts on the demographics of the workforce. People are living and keeping fit for longer and outliving the estimations of pension schemes, meaning many must stay in work for longer. As a result, many workplaces have four (or even five) generations working side by side. An increasingly diverse and inclusive workforce needs more alternative ways of working.

3. **The global pandemic:** In only a few months, the pandemic rapidly changed the way lots of people work. COVID-19 accelerated a lot of significant changes that were already happening in the economy in relation to virtual and remote working.

4. **Globalisation:** The fast pace of globalisation is also changing the face of the workforce through greater cross-border collaboration, virtual team-working and distributed workforces. Organisations can gain competitive advantages from their ability to source talent from a wide talent pool, leading to increased engagement, innovation and productivity.

5. **Business shift:** There is a driving shift from large corporations to a more entrepreneur-driven society. The rise of the gig economy has made it easier for people to take their work lives into their own hands, giving them the freedom to work when and where they want.

Why is this concerning for employees? Well, with automation, increased productivity and robots, futurist Thomas Frey estimates that two billion jobs will disappear by 2030.[7] While employees may not be able to future-proof their jobs, they can future-proof their careers. Managers and mentors need to help employees have an open mind about what the change may bring. Managers need to encourage employees to look upon change as an opportunity for growth rather than fearing the shift in status quo. When businesses adopt new technologies and automations, they free employees to perform other, more value-adding work. This is a great opportunity for employees to shine, provided they're ready to take more responsibility for their careers and are working to future-proof it. An employee's ability to be flexible and take full advantage of change will be the difference between being left behind and using it as an opportunity to develop and progress.

---

7   T Frey, *'Two Billion Jobs to Disappear by 2030'* (*Journal Environmental Health*, June 2012), www.jstor.org/stable/26329429, accessed 27 March 2023

Career paths: Myth or reality?

Predictable career paths have not existed for the past twenty to thirty years. It was different for previous generations. Then, an employee joined an organisation and followed a set path. There was an implicit promise of ongoing progression and promotion and there was the concept of a career for life. Typically, the career path was a vertical one. Career development assumed promotion into a new role, hence the concept of a career ladder with employees moving upwards as vacancies arose.

One of the challenges organisations and managers face is that employees may be looking for such a career path. They're looking for the career equivalent of a satnav. They're looking to follow a path that someone else designed, with pre-programmed routes and destinations. That type of opportunity is no longer widespread, but maybe their expectations are not a surprise, especially those that have just come out of college or university. After all, that is what they are used to. Until now, their development has been in the education system where there is a clear path. In school, every year there are some clear milestones (exams). If they pass them, they get 'promoted' by moving up to a higher class. If students go to university the same pattern follows. They pass exams at the end of the year; they go up a year. If the student passes their exams at the end of the final year, then they get their degree – a clear sign of progress and achievement accompanied by a new status with letters after their name.

Twenty years ago, progress in a corporation was not dissimilar to progress through education. Employees had fixed milestones, and if they met the requirements of those milestones, they were rewarded. This pattern still exists in professions like law and medicine. In those worlds, career development is still like climbing a ladder, one rung at a time. Perhaps it is no wonder that young employees and new graduates are looking for obvious signs of progress. They are asking, 'Where is the next milestone? When do I move up to the next level? Where is my career path?'

In many organisations, that is no longer the way careers progress. These days, organisation structures are flatter and there are fewer opportunities for promotion. During the late 1980s and early 1990s, large organisations started to downsize, flatten and restructure. As companies thinned out, leadership positions disappeared and the career ladder started to break. Some rungs disappeared and the space between others shifted from steps to leaps. The world continues to change. The ladder, if it's still there, may be harder to see and tougher to climb.

Flattened organisations and limited career ladders don't spell the end of growth or career development. Opportunities are there – different and varied – but very much there. HR professionals and people managers just need to think and talk about them differently. You need to help employees understand that even though people might like the idea of a predictable career path, the reality is quite different. There is no satnav. There aren't pre-programmed routes and destinations. In today's world, where organisations are constantly changing, career paths are more agile. In today's world, career development is much more like orienteering. It's about the employee taking the lead on deciding where they want to go and how they're going to get there. They need to understand the terrain they're in, look at the map in front of them and adjust their course as they progress.

Even if your organisation has a career framework, employees will need to take ownership of their development. It is their responsibility to develop their careers by navigating the framework, because that framework, by its very nature, is going to have to be flexible enough to evolve as the organisation grows and develops.

We need to talk about career development differently

The Oxford English Dictionary defines the word 'career' as a person's 'course or progress through life (or a distinct part of life)'. In fact, the word 'career' derives from the Latin 'carrus', referring to a chariot. Instead of a ladder, we can think about our careers as a range of experiences – large and small – that come together to shape a career journey. When we help employees think about career development as a journey rather than a ladder, it shifts their thinking:

- **They can celebrate the freedom and autonomy they have not to conform to a pre-programmed path that someone else designed:** Yes, the loss of a predictable career makes it hard to form plans, but it also allows opportunities for them to change direction and explore new options. Rather than a rigid corporate ladder, they now have a career landscape. Instead of following a set path, they're navigating the changing world around them.

- **They can focus on becoming more flexible in preparing for, and adapting to, career changes:** With this new need for people to take more responsibility for their journey, career management has become even more important. Now, career success depends not on one big decision in their twenties, but on relentlessly learning and trying new skills.

- **They will recognise that this is not new:** Unless an employee has been working for more than thirty years, they have probably never had a fixed career ladder to climb. It used to be that a person's job or career was fixed, virtually for life. That was a long time ago.

- **They can identify the strategies that have helped them navigate a changing career landscape up to now:** Reflecting on their career is likely to show that they have coped with ambiguity, tension and change very successfully before now.

To assist with this shift in thinking, I encourage you to stop defining career progression in terms of job titles, grades and promotions. Instead, focus on employability and enjoyability:

- **Employability** is an employee's capabilities, skills, knowledge, experiences, achievements and personal attributes. It is all the elements that make an employee more valuable to an employer – and thus more likely to gain employment and achieve career success. Employability creates a higher-quality workforce. It's valuable for you as a manager because you can have more flexibility resourcing business needs. At the same time, it increases employee career satisfaction. They're more satisfied because they're enhancing their experience and adding to their skillset. Help employees build and grow their capabilities through planned moves – lateral, vertical, within a function and across functions. By basing these moves on business needs, you achieve a win-win solution for both organisation and employee. Think about how you can design careers around experiences rather than jobs and positions. Careers designed around experiences emphasise the path as much as the destination, so an employee's job satisfaction increases.

- **Enjoyability** is an employee's personal experience of their working life and how much satisfaction they gain from that. Individuals are the only ones who can define what success looks like for them. Managers need to help them take ownership for deciding where they want to go and then exploring the different options for getting there. That involves exploring how they can gain more satisfaction from their current role, as well as any potential roles in the future.

The world has changed and so have careers. It's time to talk about them differently so that we can help employees understand what is needed to progress in the workplace.

2
Career Management. Whose Responsibility Is It, Anyway?

Before we start talking about who is responsible for career management, it's worth reflecting on your own experience. How has your career unfolded? Have you followed a set path determined by your organisation or has it been less predictable than that? When I started my working career thirty years ago, I was developing washing powders for P&G. There is no way I would have been able to predict that I would be sat where I am now. What about you?

When I ask clients this question, I typically get answers like 'not predictable', 'wildly unpredictable', 'always looked into opportunities and was open for change', or, 'It's been opportunistic, slow and organic'. Who is responsible for that?

Three-way partnership

There is a three-way partnership involved in career development. It involves the employee, the manager and the organisation. Employees need to be empowered to take ownership of their careers and they need to understand that it will be down to them to identify opportunities and to navigate and influence to progress. That's hard to do on their own.

They need managers and mentors to engage them in career conversations so that the connection can be made between where they're trying to get to and what the organisation needs so there can be a win-win of development that meets both the organisation's needs and the employees' needs.

The organisation needs to provide the frameworks and processes that provide that support and that structure. It needs to embrace employees' career aspirations in the talent management and development processes. (If there is an HR function, it has a critical role to play in enabling all three of these elements.)

Employee's role: Taking ownership and responsibility

Career development starts with the employee. Employees need to be empowered to take ownership of their careers. That means them investing time and effort in their professional development; demonstrating the organisation's values; building their professional opportunities and spotting or seeking out opportunities.

When we look back at our careers, we realise that they have not been predictable as we assume. They may have been opportunistic, serendipitous or organic. We may have looked for opportunities, been open to change or gone with the flow. We sometimes feel that we've had multiple careers. In essence, we have responded to what unfolded as our lives and organisations evolved. Interestingly, we're also looking back at a world that people consider was slower to change than the world as it is now and ahead of us.

Set paths have never really been how careers have unfolded, in spite of the fact that previous generations may have joined an organisation and climbed a set path or a set ladder and there was the concept of a career for life. It hasn't been like that for us and it is certainly not like that in the future.

The idea that managers and organisations can develop employees' careers is only practical in static organisations with predictable career paths. Today's organisations aren't static. They are continually changing, so this idea is outdated. Employees must develop their own careers. It's like all personal development. You can't stop smoking for someone. You can't lose weight for someone. You can't get fit for someone and you can't develop their career for them. All you can do is help them work out what they need to do and guide and support them as they take action. There are several areas employees need support with to take ownership of their careers:

- **Where they're at.** How do they feel about their current job and career situation? What are they happy with? What would they like to change? Discussing this can clarify matters and discharge some negative emotions which can get in the way of them thinking positively and taking action.

- **What's important to them in their career.** What skills do they like to use? What kind of activities do they enjoy most? What are their values in relation to work? What kind of work environment do they prefer? What kind of people do they enjoy working with?

- **What success looks like for them.** What kind of activities would they like to be doing on a day-to-day basis? Where would they be working in terms of geography or location? What kinds of responsibilities would they have? What kinds of outcomes and deliverables would they be producing? Who would they be working with and for?

- **Their skills and qualities.** What are their strengths and weaknesses? How does the organisation view them?

- **The opportunities available to them.** Are there opportunities in their current role? What about elsewhere in the organisation?

- **How to navigate the processes and politics of the organisation.** This includes understanding how the organisation works, including both processes and tactics; how to raise their profile and be more visible to key people and how to crack the system for moving jobs if that's what they want to do.

- **Identifying and evaluating different options and opportunities.** This includes looking at the pros and cons; making a decision (or at least being clearer about where they want to go) and the development or experience required.

- **Career development strategies they can use to make progress.** What actions can they take?

Some people can do this for themselves, but most of us find it a lot easier to have someone else to talk to and test our ideas on. That's where managers, mentors and HR professionals have such a valuable role to play.

Manager's role: Providing support and opportunities

I have a confession. Even with decades of leadership development experience, I have let some of my best employees down. It was when I was working at Avanade and I'll never forget it.

CASE STUDY: Julie

I had just arrived at work when one of my best employees, Julie, asked to see me. It was only 8.30am and I was surprised to see her, as I was usually the first in. I said, 'Good morning, Julie. You're in bright and early,' as I walked into my office. Within five minutes of sitting down at my computer, she put her head around the door and said, 'May I have a word, Antoinette?' Before I'd even finished saying yes, she had slid the glass door closed behind her.

Now, if you've ever managed people, you'll know that them asking to see you first thing is not normally good news. Sure enough, her eyes were full of anxiety as she said, 'I'm sorry Antoinette. I need to give you my resignation. I'm going back to Australia.' My heart sank! I was shocked. I was hurt. I was upset. I hadn't seen it coming. Yes, she was an Australian, but she'd recently married a Brit. She was happy in her work and I assumed she was settled in the UK. That was my big mistake. I *assumed* I knew what she wanted from her career, but I'd never had a conversation with her about it and she had obviously felt unable to share her wishes. It turns out she was thinking about starting a family and wanted to be close to her parents and bring her children up in her home country.

Thankfully, it wasn't too late. The company was a global company with offices in Australia. We could transfer her to an HR role in the Sydney office. She was still there ten years later, had risen to HR Director for all Asia Pacific and had two beautiful daughters. The story had a happy ending. I lost one of my best employees,

> but the company didn't. It could have been a much more positive experience for us both if we'd had that career conversation earlier. As her manager, it was down to me to start that conversation.

I'm not alone in making such assumptions. I've seen it time and again when facilitating talent review discussions. Managers assume what will make an employee happy. Managers assume their team members have the same ambitions and goals as they had when they were their age. Managers assume what would be acceptable to the employee's partner or wider family. People are all different and everyone wants different things in life. Success doesn't have to mean moving up in an organisation, taking on more responsibility, managing more people and spending a bigger budget. You will only know what employees are looking for from their careers if you ask them. Show an interest. Be curious. Show you care. The key to engaging and keeping your best people is to help them develop their careers in line with the needs of the business. The most important step you can take is show you care about your employees by talking to them about their careers.

It's like any relationship. People show they care through conversation. When managers don't have career conversations with their employees, it's like an unhappy relationship. It reaches the point where the couple no longer talk to each other about anything meaningful. Next you know, one of them has packed their bags or moved into the spare room. The same happens with employees if their career needs aren't met. They quit physically and leave. Or worse, they quit psychologically and stay.

Of course, there are other reasons that managers don't talk to employees about their careers. Those that aren't particularly focused on their employees might give lack of time as a reason. They might say that, 'employees need to take responsibility for their own careers'. And that's true – but they will do a much better job with the support of their manager. So, how can you help employees think through their aspirations? How can you help them determine what they want to share with their manager? How can you help them prepare for that conversation?

- **Don't be afraid of not having the answers:**
  Even the most caring managers can be wary of career conversations. Their biggest fear is that they won't have all the answers. They won't be able to respond to their employee's questions. That's also why employees don't make their wishes known. They don't want to express a desire that they think the company can't satisfy. The result is an unspoken standoff: managers not asking employees about their career ambitions for fear they won't have the answers and employees not sharing their career ambitions for fear they won't like the answer.

CAREER MANAGEMENT. WHOSE RESPONSIBILITY IS IT, ANYWAY?

- **Feel the fear and ask the questions anyway:**
  You won't know whether you can help employees achieve their goals unless you ask them. Ask them in such a way that you find out what's important to them. All too often, people describe success with a position or title. In other words, 'I want to be a (job title or position)', which limits their choices and possibilities. It is much more helpful to try and find out what they want their experience at work to involve, which then opens the door to all sorts of options and potential results. For example, if your employee says they want to become a team leader, ask them what it is about the team leader role that appeals to them. Is it that they want more responsibility, to gain experience of managing people or just that they want a pay rise? Once you know what it is that attracts them to the team leader role, there may be many ways of giving them that experience, even if a team leader role isn't a possibility right now.

As a manager, mentor or HR professional, you play an important role in supporting your employees' career journeys. You need to ask the right questions, provide support and guidance and identify development opportunities within the organisation. The skills and techniques you need to have effective career conversations will help you to become an even more effective people leader. Engage employees in quality career conversations and they will be empowered to take ownership of their careers and inspired to take action in a way that is right for them. Through career conversations, you can help employees develop:

- A clearer sense of career direction – not necessarily a detailed career path, but an idea of where they are going in the future.

- Increased self-insight – a more realistic view of their abilities and potential.

- A broader understanding of the career options available to them and the resources available to help them learn more.

- Increased confidence and motivation – an emotional impact which often lasts a long time.

With the increased clarity and confidence that a quality career conversation can provide, employees will be in the best possible frame of mind to share their aspirations with the organisation, discuss future career options and produce a focused and realistic development plan.

Skills and qualities for effective career conversations

There are a number of skills and qualities that are vital to ensure that you have effective career conversations with your employees:

- **Motivation and attitude:** Motivation and attitude are as important as skills. People managers must show real interest in the person, focusing on the needs of the employee and wanting them to succeed.

- **Personal qualities:** The important traits here are empathy, honesty, frankness and being non-judgemental. It also helps to be positive and enthusiastic.

- **Facilitation and coaching skills:** Keep the person in the centre of the conversation. Use effective questioning techniques, summarising, reflection and active body language to show you are being attentive.

- **Knowledge and experience:** Draw on your experience in the organisation. It could involve explaining the organisation's structure and processes or it could mean sharing knowledge about the organisation's strategy and vision.

- **Feedback skills:** Be honest and give frank, constructive feedback to stretch people outside of their comfort zone. They will gain insights that will help them identify their strengths and make progress.

Organisation's role: Facilitate and enable

At an organisational level, someone (usually the HR function) needs to take responsibility for providing the tools and resources for employees to manage their careers and for managers and mentors to support them. At the same time, managers need legitimate time and space in their roles to provide the support needed by employees.

An organisation should have a documented career management strategy that is known and understood by employees, managers and leaders. The strategy should have the explicit backing of the senior management team. There should be an identified influential person responsible for leading and sponsoring it. The strategy should cover five dimensions that are critical to effective career management within organisations:

1. **Clear definition of the organisation's values and philosophy about career development:** To create a culture that supports growth and career development, people need to be reflected in an organisation's values. They must be embedded values. They can't be lip service. They can't be aspirational. They must be used as a compass that drives action, behaviour and decision making. That means it can't just be an HR initiative. It must be a leadership decision and not just in words, but in actions.

2. **Visible sponsorship and support from senior leaders:** To support career development, you need a learning organisation and a growth culture. Having a senior leader articulate the value of career development is critical.

As role models, the stories they tell of their own career development are incredibly powerful. When Team AO work with clients, we always recommend our clients identify an executive 'Career Champion' who will sponsor and support career management within the organisation.

3. **Quality career conversations:** Every employee should have opportunities for career conversations with a manager, mentor, coach or HR professional. The individual could be internal (a member of staff) or external, provided they are trained to an appropriate level.

4. **Career development workshops, tools and support:** Employees should receive a clear message that they are responsible for managing their own careers, but they will need help in doing that. They need advice, support and training in how to reflect on their career to date to identify their skills, values and achievements. They also need guidance on how to define their ambitions and seek out or create opportunities. They need help to develop their networks and make use of the resources available to them.

5. **Links between career management, learning and development, talent management and succession planning:** Career management is a consideration at every stage of the employment lifecycle. For example, when recruiting and

onboarding new employees, managers need to make it clear that the organisation treats career development as important.

Good career management is critical. It is the key to employability. It is about showing employees there are options available to them in the organisation whatever their role and career stage. It's about helping them take the actions to progress and develop within their current role and beyond.

If you would like to assess your current situation, our Career Management Culture Health Check is a free, quick and easy online tool that will provide you with a starting point and show where your organisation is strong and where attention is needed to improve: www.antoinetteoglethorpe.com/resources/career-management-culture-health-check.

3
Why Career Conversations Are Important

The main purpose of a career conversation is to help a person explore their career options. It helps them identify both the skills and experience they already have and those they will need. It then helps them to create a plan to achieve their career goals that are mutually beneficial to themselves and their organisation.

Are career conversations even necessary?

All organisations are under a certain amount of pressure. They're under pressure to grow. They're under pressure to maximise performance. They're under pressure to deliver results. However, there's a challenge. While organisations want to maximise employees' performance, employees want to maximise their careers. These goals are not one and the same.

Years of change, restructuring, outsourcing and down-sizing have caused people to take a more active role in managing their careers. Employees at all levels face various career decisions daily, for example:

- What opportunities are there for development and progression?

- Will I stay or leave?

- Will I change careers?

- Will I pursue new projects?

- Will I obtain another qualification?

- Will I start up on my own?

In a rapidly changing work environment, the answers are not always obvious. It is in the context of this eco-nomic reality that helping employees to develop their careers assumes more significance, not less. Career management is about getting people to where they want to be and where the organisation needs them to be. If you want your people to be committed to the organisation, engaged with their work and driven to perform, you need to provide them with the tools and resources they need to manage their careers within the organisation.

Organisations sometimes focus so much on what employees need to do to meet the needs of the business that they lose sight of what the organisation needs to do to meet employees' needs. Yet, this is crucial if you are going to be effective in retaining and developing talent within the organisation.

Career development is a tricky area for organisations. This is because it deals with the future and is a venture into the unknown. It is also deeply personal. Many managers worry that asking about careers may unsettle staff or even make them leave, but evidence shows that attending to career issues makes staff more loyal to the organisation and more productive.[8]

Meaningfulness of work and the fit between a person and their job are two of the key drivers of engagement at work. Support your employees in managing their careers and they will feel connected to their work. They will feel valued for their contribution and motivated to contribute further. Their willingness to apply and increase their capability will be enhanced.

Career management in organisations is important whatever the state of the employment market. In a buoyant job market, it's often easier for employees to leave a company than to manage their career internally. If the organisation doesn't develop their careers,

---

8   LinkedIn, '2018 Workplace Learning Report' (LinkedIn, 2018), https://learning.linkedin.com/resources/workplace-learning-report-2018, accessed 27 March 2023

they quit physically and leave. In a tough economy, the bigger risk is that employees quit psychologically and stay! Supporting your employees in managing their careers isn't just a 'nice thing to do' – it's a business imperative.

Not having career conversations can be costly

Before I set up my own business, I worked for a global insurance company as the Leadership and Organisation Development (LOD) Director. I was responsible for the talent management process. After months of preparation, it was time to chair the talent review meeting. Our aim was to agree the succession plan for the executive board. As is usual in these kinds of meetings, various senior people sat around a board table. Their task was to slot names into the boxes on the succession plan. My job was to facilitate the discussion and encourage challenge and debate.

The Board agreed on most names easily, but a minority caused much discussion. For example, the suggested successor for the Head of Property Underwriting in London was a well-respected underwriter in the Bermudian office, and there was full agreement about his ability and potential. As always, I asked how the employee in question would feel about such a move. His manager's response? 'Don't worry, love. He'll be made up. He's a good, ambitious bloke. His wife doesn't work and his kids aren't at school yet, so there won't be any issue with him moving to London.'

Six months later, the Head of Property Underwriting left the company as part of a reorganisation. Consequently, his successor got the fated tap on the shoulder. How do you think he responded? He said, 'No thanks. I've never wanted the management responsibility that comes with being a head of department and my wife won't leave her family in Bermuda.' The whole succession plan fell over because it hadn't considered the career wishes of the employee involved. If you've ever been on the receiving end of a job move that you didn't want or expect, you'll know how he felt. You may also empathise with what the employee did next. He decided that since the company clearly had a different view of his future to his own, he would be better off leaving.

It is hard to predict the true cost of a departing employee. There are many intangible and often untracked costs associated with employee turnover. A study by the Center for American Progress concluded the cost of losing an employee can be anywhere from 16% of the annual salary of an employee paid hourly, to 213% of the salary of a highly trained position.[9] If we assume the Bermudian Property Underwriter was making $100,000 a year, the true loss could be up to

---

9   H Boushey & SJ Glynn, 'There Are Significant Business Costs to Replacing Employees' (Center for American Progress, 16 November 2012), www.americanprogress.org/article/there-are-significant-business-costs-to-replacing-employees, accessed 22 March 2023

$213,000 to the company. All for the lack of a short conversation about careers.

This story is only too common, and it highlights a major risk: if you don't talk to employees about their careers, you can't take their ambitions into account. If you don't consider those ambitions in your people processes, you could be wasting your time and energy.

Benefits of great career conversations

On a more positive note, there are enormous benefits that employees can gain from having effective career conversations. Those include:

- Helping them feel more satisfied and motivated in their current role, no matter what their ambitions.

- Encouraging them to identify development opportunities and take steps that will help them to be more effective.

- Having conversations that make them want to stay with the organisation rather than go elsewhere.

- Having a flexible approach, which means they take ownership of their career development.

- Supporting their wellbeing by taking a holistic approach to growth and development.

There are also enormous benefits that managers and the organisation can gain, and they largely relate to building agile, adaptable and future-proof organisations:

1. **Alignment between the ambitions of the organisation and the ambitions of the individual.** In today's disruptive marketplace, leaders must develop their employees to grasp market opportunities. Career conversations allow organisations to adjust roles in a way that will take advantage of people's strengths. They also allow adjustments that respond to people's interests and aspirations to create a more agile response to organisation development. It allows employees to identify and explore the alignment between their goals and those of their organisation. In turn, this increases commitment, loyalty and the pool of internal talent available to the organisation.

2. **Resourcing new projects, roles and responsibilities.** In times of change and growth, effective resourcing and redeployment of skills is more important than ever. Career conversations raise an employee's awareness of their interests, strengths, values and aspirations. That can help decisions around promotions. It can also inform resourcing decisions related to secondments, project work and lateral moves. Career conversations help move people into roles where their skills are most suited and their aspirations are best met.

3. **Growing future leaders and specialists.** Career conversations help employees develop skills the business requires now and in the future. Most highly skilled jobs need skills that are specific to the organisation or are hard to recruit. Effective career conversations will also allow employees to be better prepared for new roles. That means the transition into a new role will be smoother and more successful. Career conversations can also help employees understand how their role might change with time. They can then identify and develop skills in readiness for these changes. In this way, career conversations can be a powerful tool for building agile, adaptable and future-proof organisations.

4. **Attracting and retaining talented employees.** Career conversations help companies attract and keep high-performing employees. Ambitious employees look for career coaching and development support. That makes regular career conversations an attractive component of any employee experience strategy. Employees are more likely to remain with their current employer when offered the opportunity to develop. When career conversations don't happen, employees are more likely to leave an organisation. In a global market where skilled workers are in short supply, these practices become even more important.

5. **Increased organisation performance.** Get career conversations right and individuals will feel connected to their work. They will feel valued for their contribution and engaged with the organisation, so they will be more motivated to contribute. Their willingness to apply and increase their capability will be enhanced. If each employee performs better and is assisted to reach their full potential, the organisation is more likely to reach its goals.

In summary, career conversations can help build an organisation's capability to meet future demands. They help keep existing staff, as well as attract high-quality applicants. This unlocks a value chain. By having a career conversation, a manager can improve employee performance, drive organisation performance, increase business results and, ultimately, serve their community better.

PART 2
EFFECTIVE CAREER CONVERSATIONS

Career conversations are powerful conversations that touch on an employee's life outside as well as inside the workplace. For that reason, many managers are nervous of having career conversations in case they don't have the positive impact they intend. In this section, we'll look at those factors that make a career conversation effective. Powerful questions are critical and we will explore how to make them powerful. Finally, I will provide an overview of the Career Conversation Model and the career conversation tools that support it.

4
What Makes A Career Conversation Effective?

It's a sad fact that people can usually identify a memorably bad career conversation more easily than a good one. It's often hard for people to recall a career conversation which was of significant value to them. Remember that time at the end of a not particularly glowing performance appraisal when your boss asked you where you wanted to be in five years? All you could think was, 'Anywhere but here working for you!' So, you just looked at them blankly and you could see in their eyes that they were really frustrated with you. Horrible at the time (thank goodness you don't work for them anymore), but when you think about it a bit more, you'll realise that you've had many other more positive conversations about your career. That is why Team AO ask people in our Career Conversations workshops to think about a valuable career conversation.

CASE STUDY: Cath

Cath worked in an engineering company and said that probably the most important career conversation she'd had was an informal one. After school, she'd decided she was going to do civil engineering, but since it was so male dominated, she thought she wouldn't be able to cope. She ended up in a job that she didn't enjoy and didn't feel respected for. She felt that she had to do something else, so she had a conversation with her partner and they went through all the roles she was potentially interested in. Her final choices came down to physiotherapy or environmental engineering. It was tough to choose between two options that are so different, but her partner helped her find opportunities to try out what working in each of those areas might be like so that she had a sense of what she was getting herself into. She eventually chose the environmental engineering route.

Cath's story highlights several characteristics that make a career conversation effective. The following are ones that come up time and again:

1. **They are not necessarily with 'the boss'.**
   The most effective career conversations are not necessarily with the boss. The fundamental priority is that the person holding the conversation is objective. They have the best interests of the individual at heart and no underlying agenda. For those reasons, career

conversations can be difficult for the immediate line manager. Career conversations do eventually need to take place between employees and their managers, but that might be a better place to finish rather than start the conversation.

2. **They often take place informally.** Good career conversations often take place outside any formal management or HR process, or they may take place in what we might call 'semi-formal' settings. Such settings include mentoring discussions, regular progress meetings and follow-up meetings after an appraisal. Although good conversations can take place as part of formal HR processes, they're not all that frequent.

3. **They are sometimes unplanned.** Some meetings where good career conversations take place are planned, but they can also be spontaneous and unplanned. Valuable conversations with friends and work colleagues, for example, often happen spontaneously.

4. **They don't have to take a long time.** Good career conversations usually take time, say three-quarters of an hour to an hour. Sometimes, a short first conversation is useful as a prelude to setting up a longer meeting. While a single conversation on its own can be pivotal, sometimes people need several conversations to make progress.

5. **They provide different levels of support at different times.** Employees often need career support at defining points in their career. For example, starting a new role, considering a job move or when they come to the end of a development programme. At other times, they need a lighter touch.

Most of all, it's all about the employee and what they want from their working life. They have to feel the focus is on them and that their future hasn't already been decided by others.

Why performance reviews are *not* the place for career conversations

You may feel comfortable that your organisation isn't neglecting these important conversations. After all, you ask about careers as part of the performance review. You have a question that asks employees, 'What are your career goals?' This is a common way for organisations to address career conversations if they recognise their importance, but I'm sorry to tell you that this approach doesn't work. If you have them to hand, look at some completed performance reviews. In how many of them is that question answered? One HR business partner told me that in her case, the question was left blank in at least 80% of cases. In the other 20% of cases, the box was ticked or had a generic statement like 'To be promoted'.

Why don't employees answer the question? Research for the Department for Business, Innovation and Skills[10] confirms what we know instinctively. Career choices and decisions are complex. They're influenced by many factors – both internal and external. A question such as, 'What are your career goals?' is simple to ask, but not at all simple for most people to answer (unless they have done a lot of thinking about it beforehand).

Even if they can answer the question, the last few minutes of a performance review is almost the worst place to tackle such a complex subject. A performance review focuses on an employee's *past* performance over a period of time. The emphasis is on accomplishments relative to specific standards set by the organisation. A career conversation, on the other hand, focuses on *future*. The emphasis is on the skills and abilities needed to achieve personal career goals. Managers and employees need to be having career conversations separate to the performance reviews.

The importance of a growth mindset for career development

Another feature of effective career conversations is that they encourage a growth mindset rather than

10   Department for Business Innovation and Skills, 'Adult Career Decision-Making: Qualitative Research' (Gov.UK, 18 September 2013), www.gov.uk/government/publications/adult-career-decision-making-qualitative-research, accessed 22 March 2023

a fixed one. Adaptability has always played a key role in workplace success. Now, more than ever, it seems like careers require us to be constantly evolving. The pace of change is accelerating. To succeed in any industry and to be ready to take part in the next evolution, professionals must grow and develop. According to a report by McKinsey, up to 375 million workers worldwide will need to change roles or learn new skills by 2030.[11]

One challenge to growth and career development in organisations is that many employees assume they are not capable. They tell themselves, 'I'm not a leader,' or, 'I'm not very creative,' or, 'Spreadsheets are not my strong suit.' Even worse, some managers assume their employees are not capable and don't have potential to progress. According to renowned Stanford psychologist Carol Dweck, we can take control of our own development with the right mindset. In her 2007 book *Mindset: The New Psychology of Success*,[12] Dweck calls this having a 'growth' mindset (vs a 'fixed' one). She says that it's not intelligence, talent or education that sets successful people apart. It's their mindset, or the way that they approach life's challenges.

---

11   McKinsey & Company, 'Jobs Lost, Jobs Gained: Workforce Transitions in A Time of Automation' (McKinsey Global Institute, December 2017), www.mckinsey.com/~/media/ BAB489A30B724BECB5DEDC41E9BB9FAC.ashx, accessed 23 March 2023

12   C Dweck, *Mindset: The New Psychology of Success* (Random House, 28 February 2006)

Mindset, Dweck says, is the view that you adopt for yourself that determines the way you live your life, see the world and make decisions. It is essentially your perspective, or the way you view the world. In short, it's the way your perceptions or your beliefs about your abilities and qualities shape the way you operate. Dweck describes the simple, yet impactful differences between the two mindsets:

People with a fixed mindset believe they 'are who they are' and were born with a set level of talent, intelligence and even interests, so they're more likely to seek out opportunities and situations that affirm these views. For example, they will repeat the same job to receive praise and believe that talent (not effort) is the source of their success. They are keenly interested to know whether they have succeeded or failed but they give up easily and ignore useful, constructive feedback. They don't believe they can improve, so they don't try to. They tend to avoid challenges. Striving for success and avoiding failure at all costs become a way of maintaining their sense of being smart or skilled.

People with a growth mindset believe they can develop their abilities, so they invest energy in learning. They're more likely to seek out situations to experiment and see failure as an opportunity to grow. They seek input from others, try different strategies and gain insights from their mistakes. By seeking opportunities, people with a growth mindset succeed and achieve more in their careers. Belief leads to action, which in turn leads to success. That success reinforces the belief, so it creates a virtuous circle of progress.[13]

When it comes to developing their careers, people with different mindsets are likely to respond differently. A fixed mindset employee will be more likely to resist career conversations. They may say they're happy in their current role and don't want to progress. They'll stick to doing the job they know and working with people and techniques they're familiar with. They will be averse to trying new opportunities because they want to avoid challenge for fear of failure. A growth mindset employee, on the other hand, believes that they can develop their talents and abilities. They'll be more likely to engage in career conversations and search out opportunities. They will try new challenges and responsibilities, even though they may not be good at them right away. They know it will take work and it might not be the right choice, but they'll learn from the experience anyway and progress in the long run. The marriage of growth mindset with a commitment to learning is a powerful combination for career development.

Encouraging a growth mindset

Most people operate with both fixed and growth mindsets. The key is to understand when a fixed mindset is holding someone back and to help them

---

13 For further information on Dweck's ideas: www.mindsetworks.com, accessed 22 March 2023

become more 'growth' minded. Here are some ways to value and encourage a growth mindset:

1. **Think lattice, not ladder:** The traditional view of career development involves climbing the corporate ladder. That's a fixed mindset view. 'I've only progressed if I get a promotion. If I don't, I haven't made any progress at all.' That isn't true. Career growth is deciding on what success looks like for the individual and how they're going to move towards that. It's about helping employees have an experience at work that feels positive and rewarding. It's about developing their skills and employability. Be creative. Provide opportunities for development within their role and through special projects and assignments.

2. **Focus on progression, not perfection:** Encourage employees to accept their imperfections. Help them work on improving and developing their skills – especially those they find hard. Don't write them off just because they're not the best at something. Be confident in their ability to adapt and improve. Build their confidence by helping them reflect on what they've learned and the progress they've already made. Employees can get so focused on developing a skill that they forget to step back and see how much they've grown during the process. Make a point to recognise and celebrate their achievements – even if they're not quite where they want to be yet.

3. **Remember, 'not yet' doesn't mean 'not ever':** Viewing performance as binary (pass/fail or right/wrong) is a breeding ground for fixed mindsets and to be avoided. One way to do this is to embrace the power of 'not yet'. Viewing lack of achievement as a 'failure' puts employees nowhere. Viewing it as 'not yet' puts them on a trajectory towards success and tells them that they've made progress and can continue to grow their abilities. Encourage them to think of failure as part of the learning process – a difficult task will challenge them and ultimately help them develop.

4. **Value the journey not just the destination:** Put the priority on experimenting, exploring and growing. Encourage employees to enjoy the entire process and not just focus on the success of the outcome. There's nothing more valuable than learning from experience. While they do need to spend time researching and learning a new skill, also encourage them to put that skill into action. Give them those opportunities. If they hold back until they're 100% ready, they'll never act.

5. **See feedback as a gift:** Provide feedback on a regular basis. Don't just give praise. Use the approach of 'Yes… and' to celebrate success and explore what they can do to improve. Present comments constructively rather than judgementally so they know you want to help them improve.

6. **Share your experience:** Mentor and guide your direct reports and other employees as they navigate their careers. Help by challenging them and imparting your hard-earned wisdom. It's invaluable for them to be able to learn from someone who's been there, done that and can help them avoid potential issues.

How to have a great career conversation

There are several factors that contribute to a great career conversation:

- **Focus on who the employee is, what they want and why.** A good career conversation cuts through the noise to help employees focus on where they're at and reduce unnecessary stress. Discussing how they feel about their current job and career clarifies matters, which can help them unload negative emotions.

- **Help them reflect on their experience.** What skills do they like to use? What activities do they enjoy most? What are their values in relation to work? What work environment do they prefer? What people do they enjoy working with?

- **Enable them to gain clarity of direction.** In an effective career conversation, people will reflect on what their ambitions really are. What does success look like for them? Helping them connect their personal values and career wishes will ignite their passion, which triggers the desire to develop.

- **Develop self-awareness by holding up a mirror.** Good career conversations build confidence. Hold up a mirror so individuals can reflect on their skills and performance, thinking about the feedback they've received from others in the organisation. They then identify what their strengths and weaknesses are themselves.

- **Enable a change of perspective.** An effective career conversation challenges individuals to think differently, helping them move out of their comfort zone and consider what opportunities are available to them. Those opportunities might be in their current role or elsewhere in the organisation.

- **Aid their decision making.** Quality career conversations help individuals evaluate different alternatives and opportunities, look at the pros and cons and make a decision (or at least gain greater clarity about where they want to go and the development they need to get there).

- **Build networks and organisational understanding.** People often need support in navigating the processes and politics of the organisation. Career conversations can help them develop an understanding of how people succeed 'around here' and decide how to raise their profile and be more visible to key people. They can also help them work out how to crack the system for moving to a different role if that's what they want to do.

- **End with action.** Good conversations usually lead to action by focusing on the 'What?' What career development strategies can employees use to make progress? What actions can they take? Agree on how you're going to check in and review progress.

By making a point of focusing on these factors, managers make those career conversations more valuable to the employee and to the organisation. At the end of the day, the best way for managers to have effective career conversations is to go into them with a growth mindset and positive intent to empower the employee's career development. The more they think about it ahead of time and the more they prepare, the more likely it is to run smoothly and yield results that are as positive as possible.

5
The Power Is In
The Question

Self-awareness is a constant process throughout your lifetime. It requires some careful thought and reflection. It can't be achieved by reading a book or blog post. Quite the contrary, if an employee is going to become more self-aware, they will have to be willing to get down and do some hard work. The Oxford Dictionary defines self-awareness as 'conscious knowledge of one's own character, feelings, motives and desires'.

In a business context, this sounds rather soft. You might think it is only relevant if someone's professional aspirations are to be a psychologist or HR professional. You may think it is not as critical as the 'hard stuff' like experience, skills or credentials after your name. That's not the case.

I have three decades of experience as a leader and businesswoman. I have worked in diverse industries from fast moving consumer goods to consultancy to technology services to education. My experience is that self-awareness is one of the most important factors for career success. If employees are going to take ownership of their career development, they need to increase their self-awareness and knowledge of skills for career growth. Here are some of the key self-awareness questions employees need to be able to answer:

- What are your strengths?

- What are your weaknesses?

- What are your values and motivations?

- What elements would a role need to include for you to feel satisfied at the end of a day's work?

- What are you curious about?

- What are you interested in?

- What triggers stress you and how do you cope with them?

- What inspires you?

- What derails you?

- What is your communication style?

- How do you manage conflict?

- How do you respond to authority?

- How do you deal with criticism?

As someone who'll be asking these questions, it's perhaps pertinent to take some time to consider them yourself. How many of them are you personally able to answer?

Why self-awareness is important to career success

To appreciate the role of self-awareness in career development, it is important to understand careers in the 21st century. The world of work is more dynamic and chaotic than ever. In previous generations, a person would generally accept a job and hold onto it throughout the entire duration of their careers. Those days are over and done with, as I shared in Chapter 1. These days, the trend is toward self-managed careers. In other words, it's down to individuals to take ownership of their career development. People have also become more mindful of the impact of family and lifestyle issues on their careers. Employees want to have a more flexible approach to their career development and to their own career development plans. That relies on a thorough awareness of their interests, values, talents and lifestyle preferences. They can then set appropriate career goals and develop appropriate career strategies. A higher level of self-awareness can help individuals achieve the following:

- **Increased contribution:** When an employee knows themself, they know their strengths. This gives them a better understanding of the unique qualities they bring to their interactions with others and to their work. They can lean on their strengths during difficult times to help them, and others, get through the challenges. Understanding themselves is a vital part of learning to be proactive, creative and innovative. When a person understands themself, they can use their imagination and intuition to address challenges. Self-aware employees use their talents to start initiatives rather than complain or criticise.

- **Professional growth:** When employees are self-aware, they also know the areas they wish to develop. This is important to continue to grow professionally. Self-awareness is an important part of career development because it forces an employee to look at themselves objectively. Examining their strengths, weaknesses, successes and failures is enlightening. It can help them determine what works and what doesn't. They can then move forward with a fresh perspective and ambitions.

- **Ability to influence their reputation:** Self-awareness makes it easier for an employee to understand how others see them. This is key for success. It's essential to be aware of the perceptions of their bosses, of course. It's also important for them to know how they come across when they're working as a team member or leader.

- **Greater job satisfaction:** By focusing on what makes the employee feel happy and valued, they can find roles that are most satisfying. Understanding their specific talents and areas of expertise can help them find the opportunities where they can shine.

Powerful questions engage and empower employees

Helping employees develop their self-awareness relies on powerful questions. Let me give you an example from my own experience.

CASE STUDY: Ian

One of my clients worked in a Mental Health Trust. Ian was coming up to fifty-five, which meant he could take retirement if he wanted. I must admit, it felt strange talking about retirement to someone who looked so young. He was silver-haired, but in that George Clooney kind of way and was tall, athletic and healthy looking. However, he was torn. Mental health is a demanding line of work. The Trust was going through a lot of change, there were all sorts of staff issues and he was tired.

I said to him, 'Suppose we wave a magic wand and we're transported forwards in time to your perfect retirement party. What would people be saying about you in their speeches?' We spent the best part of an hour exploring that question. We focused on the different people that would be at the party – his bosses, his colleagues, his team members, the service users, his friends and family. At the end he said, 'You know what? I'm not finished yet. The work is hard and it is tiring. I've achieved a lot, but there's still a couple of things I want to make happen if I'm going to leave a legacy. Actually, reminding myself of those and reminding myself of why I do this work has got me quite excited.'

That's the impact of powerful questions.

Problem-focused vs solution-focused questions

There are two distinct approaches you can take to raise awareness. You can ask problem-focused questions, or you can ask solution-focused questions. Let me explain the difference. Typically, when you want to solve a problem or create change, you use problem-focused questions which raise awareness of what's wrong, why it's wrong, weaknesses to fix and how to solve what's wrong. For linear problems such as fixing a puncture on a bicycle, a broken leg or even an aeroplane, the problem-focused approach works very well. Find the cause of the problem (eg, the hole in the inner tube), fix that cause and the problem goes away. When working with people and careers, the problem-focused approach is less effective. For example, when someone is dissatisfied with their work, they may be clear on what they're not happy with (their boss, their workload, their colleagues, the lack of resources, etc), but as we've seen time and again, focusing on problems doesn't necessarily help change the situation. In fact, focusing on it often makes the matter worse.

If we take a traditional, problem-focused approach to career conversations, our tendency is to focus on all the 'mistakes' made and challenges encountered, all the aspects that aren't liked and aren't working and the dreaded situation if nothing changes. Such an approach is debilitating and disempowering. Solution-focused questions offer an empowering alternative. They raise awareness of what's wanted (the 'solution'), what's working, strengths to build on and next steps. With this approach, it's possible for everyone to make progress. When someone is dissatisfied with their work, they can focus on how they would like it to be different, what's working well and all the skills and resources they can use to build on that. A solution-focused approach to career conversations helps employees focus on all the achievements they are proud of and have contributed to progress, what they like and are good at already and what they want and desire.

When we want people to take ownership for their career and their development, we want them to use energy, creativity and inspiration. Approaching the challenge of career development in our traditional problem-focused way closes down conversation, it limits opportunity and creativity and it all feels somewhat futile and debilitating. This is the opposite of what we want. Instead, we want people to be empowered. The solution-focused approach is more effective because it opens up possibilities. It's a lot more fun and it energises people.

Solution-focused questions specifically ask about positives. What does the employee like about their current role? What would they like to do more of? What strengths do they feel they bring? What value do they contribute to the organisation? Such questions provoke reflection, insight, ideas and action. They keep the focus on the employee while helping them see the situation differently. I like the phrase, 'change the viewing, change the doing'. In other words, by helping them see the situation in a new light, you help them take the actions needed to create change. You help them recognise possibilities. You encourage them to create many alternatives and achievable action steps to build on their knowledge of how to progress.

Adapted from the work of Mark McKergow, co-author of the book The Solutions Focus: Making Coaching and Change SIMPLE,[14] we use the activity below to help managers recognise the value of solution-focused questions.

---

14 P Z Jackson and M McKergow, *The Solutions Focus: Making Coaching and Change SIMPLE* (Nicholas Brealey International, 2nd edition, 14 December 2006)

ACTIVITY: Problem-focused vs solution-focused questions

Think of something you'd like to be better at – maybe a sport or hobby – something where the stakes aren't too high, but you have definite interest in making progress. There are two sets of questions to answer. You can get a friend to ask you the questions or just write the answers on a piece of paper. The idea is for you to compare the effects of the two sets. It's important you spend the same length of time on each set of questions. I suggest three minutes (you might like to use a timer). Answer as many as you have time for in the first set before moving on to the second set after three minutes and finishing after six minutes.

Set 1: Problem-focused questions

- What is the problem?
- How long has it been a problem?
- When has this problem been at its worst?
- What are the main causes of this problem?
- What are the barriers to success?
- How are you going to solve this problem?

Set 2: Solution-focused questions

- What are you aiming to achieve?
- What would be happening if everything went perfectly?
- What are you doing well already?
- What is the very best you have ever done?
- What went well on that occasion?

- What small step could you take to build on this success?
- How would other people know that things were improving?

Hopefully your answers helped you discover that the solution-focused approach opens more possibilities – and can be a whole lot more fun!

When Team AO run this activity, we often hear that focusing on the problem led to self-blame and thinking about what people are not good at. The solution-focused questions put an individual in a more positive frame of mind, spark more thought and are more empowering and energising.

Effective career conversations rely on powerful questions. Asking solution-focused questions can help managers to have a more positive, actionable conversation. They will increase the emotive response to answer such questions and therefore increase the chance that the employee will share information. This will hopefully lead the employee to take ownership of their career development as well as improve their understanding of how their manager can help them reach their goals.

For career conversations, the most powerful questions are strengths-based and solution-focused. The Career Conversation Model and the Career

Conversation Toolkit that I'm going to share with you in the next chapters are designed to use a solution-focused approach to encourage, empower and engage employees so that they are more creative in their thinking and take ownership for their careers.

6
Career Conversation Model

Typically, people want three outputs from a career conversation: (1) Information about new opportunities, different roles and career development options; (2) Feedback on their skills and performance and how the organisation views their potential, and (3) Guidance about possible career paths, growth opportunities and development options.

You will notice that with this in mind, your employee's expectations of their career conversation may be that you will have all the answers. That's not the case. Effective career conversations put the employee in the driving seat. Your role is to empower them to come up with the options and decisions that are right for them within your organisation.

In the last chapter, we talked about the power of a good question. As a manager, you don't have to have all the answers, but you do have to have the questions that will help them discover those answers for themselves. This is one of the areas that most managers would like help with. The most frequently asked questions in our Confident Career Conversations workshops relate to tools. Questions like:

- What effective tools could I use in my career conversations?

- Are there any particular tools you use that lead to great insights and actions?

- What tools can I use to enable employees to change their view on development?

Unless you are an experienced and qualified professional coach (and even when you are), it can be hard to always have the right question at your fingertips. I created the Career Conversation Model and Career Conversation Toolkit to do the heavy lifting for you. The Career Conversation Model gives you a flexible framework to structure and hold an effective career conversation. The Career Conversation Toolkit gives you a set of practical, solution-focused questions for each part of the framework. As with any toolkit, different tools serve different purposes and help you achieve different outcomes. The toolkit is designed to provide you with the flexibility to handle different situations. A career conversation can be very broad in its reach and may cover some or all the following:

1. **Feelings about work.** How does the employee feel about their current job and career? Discussion can help discharge any negative emotions which can get in the way of positive thought and action.

2. **Skills and reputation.** Feedback on how they are doing and how the organisation views them.

3. **Values, drivers and ambitions.** What's important to them in their career? What are their values in relation to work? What does success look like?

4. **Career options.** What opportunities are available to them (in their current role and elsewhere in the organisation)?

5. **Processes and politics of the organisation.** Do they understand how to get work done 'around here'? How can they raise their profile and be more visible?

6. **Evaluating different options and opportunities.** Looking at the pros and cons and deciding (or at least being clearer about) where they want to go.

7. **Next steps.** What career development strategies can they use to make progress? What actions can they take?

Eight stages of a great career conversation

1. Take time to prepare. If you don't know the individual, see if they are happy to send you their CV or their LinkedIn profile. Tell them in advance if there are questions you would like them to think about. Emphasise that the conversation is confidential.

2. Set up the conversation. It can be helpful to frame these conversations by managing expectations. That means emphasising that the individual is responsible for managing their career. Your role is simply to help them manage it better.

3. Establish trust. Establishing trust is a process and one that can't necessarily be achieved in a few minutes. You probably already have a relationship with the individual, so the trust might already be there. If it's a new relationship, then you might want to take time to establish trust before you ask them to open up. A lot of that trust building might be achieved through sharing information about your own career and experience.

4. Agree on the desired outcomes from the conversation. Establish an open feel to the conversation. Put the other person at ease. Show your interest, listen carefully and check that you understand what they say to you.

5. Explore the situation from their perspective. Exploring the situation from the employee's perspective is where the Career Conversation Model and Toolkit really come into their own. In the next sections, I'll describe what they are and how best to use them.

6. Share information. In a career conversation, employees are often looking to you for guidance and information. When you want to empower an employee, you need to be very careful in the way you share information. You want to resist giving advice, but you probably do have some useful experience to share. The secret is to share your own insights in such a way that they can be rejected. When someone has chosen to talk to you about their career or sees you as a mentor, they have awarded you a degree of authority and respect. They are likely to see your insights as 'expert advice', even if you don't intend them that way. To avoid that, you need to make sure they feel comfortable rejecting them. Here are some ideas on how to do that:

- **Ask permission.** For example, 'Would you like a suggestion?' It's unlikely they'll say no, but at least you've shown that it is a suggestion, not direction.

- **Use a caveat.** When telling a story from your own experience, a useful preface is, 'This may not work for you, but what I did was…'

- **Offer ideas from a third party.** You might say, 'I knew someone who always tackled this kind of challenge like this…' This has the advantage that the employee is likely to reject ideas more easily if the third party isn't in the room.

- **Offer ideas from a remote source.** An example is, 'John Lees has written many articles on this subject and his suggestion would probably be…' This gives the idea expert credibility, but they can still reject it if it doesn't fit.

Try to meet the individual's needs for information, including opportunities outside the organisation. Where appropriate, suggest other people to talk to. Use your own and others' careers to illustrate options but don't expect the individual to want a career like yours.

7. Agree on actions. Finally, you want to agree on actions. Those actions might be observational, like reflecting on what they've enjoyed about their work that day. Maybe they'll go and talk to other people. Maybe they'll research options. Maybe they'll make a decision. Ultimately, if they're going to be taking ownership, you want them to do something because of the conversation.

8. Close the conversation. Leave enough time to bring the discussion to a close and agree on what happens next. Ensure the individual knows they can come back to you.

The Career Conversation Model

The Career Conversation Model helps you to structure your conversations to make the most of every moment and to help the individual to come up with their own solutions. It assumes that the best career decisions combine past-, present- and future-thinking. Career conversations can help people integrate hindsight from their past experience with foresight about where they could go in the future. Bringing both together determines action that can be taken in the present. The model explores three parts of a person's career journey:

1. Past: Where they've come from and the lessons they have already learned along the way.

2. Future: Where they are going to and the routes they could take to get there.

3. Present: Where they are right now and the small changes they could take to set them on course for success.

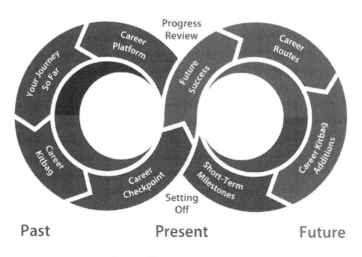

Career Conversation Model

The Career Conversation Toolkit

The Career Conversation Toolkit provides a set of tools for each stage of the Career Conversation Model. Drawing on principles of positive psychology, solution focus and neuroscience, the Career Conversation Toolkit gives managers, mentors and coaches a set of thoughtfully conceived questions to:

1. Provoke reflection, insight, ideas and action.

2. Keep the focus on the employee.

3. Encourage them to take ownership of their career progress.

The questions are packaged into ten different tools, each of which relates to a stage in the Career Conversation Model. To make it easy to use, the toolkit has been designed as a set of cards where each tool has a conversation card. The cards provide a practical but flexible framework that can be used as the basis for a conversation that is twenty minutes or less. You can use one tool or a few tools in whatever sequence or order makes sense for the individual and their situation.

The tools are simple and straightforward, but very effective. As discussed in the previous chapter, the questions are carefully designed to 'change the viewing and change the doing'. In other words, the tools help the employee see the situation differently by acknowledging progress so far, identifying what's already working, detailing the preferred outcome, highlighting existing resources and building employee self-efficacy. That, in turn, helps the employee to develop new behaviours. The tools help them recognise possibilities and turn challenges into platforms for opportunities. They encourage them to generate multiple options and identify small, achievable actions. They help them find ways to build on their existing knowledge of how to progress.

For any conversation to be effective, it's important that it's natural and not scripted. I see these tools like recipe cards. When you're new to cooking or lack confidence, it's useful to have some clear instructions that can keep you safe if you follow them to the letter. However, they are simply a starting point. The idea is that as you become more skilled, experienced and confident, these questions form a guideline and framework which you can adapt to your own taste.

The ten conversation tools

The questions are packaged into ten different tools. Each tool consists of five powerful, solution-focused questions:

1. **Career platform:** Helps an employee determine what they want to change in their career and motivates them to take action.

2. **Your journey so far:** Allows employees to reflect on what they're good at, what's most important to them and how they like to work.

3. **Career kitbag:** Helps employees identify all the resources they have that will help them make progress. Skills include technical skills, soft skills and career development skills.

4. **Future success:** Helps employees articulate their ambitions by describing what success will look like.

5. **Career routes:** Helps employees identify the options available to them in their current role and/or in new roles.

6. **Career kitbag additions:** Helps employees analyse the skills, experiences, information and relationships that they need to develop, to progress towards their future success.

7. **Career checkpoint:** Connects employees' ambition with reality to identify how their current situation is satisfying their aspirations and the progress they have made.

8. **Short-term milestones:** Helps employees focus on an achievable goal in the not-too-distant future.

9. **Setting off:** Encourages employees to commit to do-able actions that will help them make progress, however small.

10. **Progress review:** Helps employees learn from the experience.

PART 3
CAREER CONVERSATION TOOLKIT

Saying that managers should have career conversations with their employees is one thing, but what tools can a manager use to facilitate these conversations? In this section we will take an in-depth look at the Career Conversation Toolkit. You will gain a practical understanding of how managers can use them in career conversations to ensure they're equipped with everything they need to support their employees and their career planning.

7
Learning From The Past

In this chapter we're going to look at the three career conversation tools that focus on the past: the *Career Platform* tool, the *Your Journey So Far* tool and the *Career Kitbag* tool. These three tools help employees identify what they already know about developing their careers in an organisation. They help them look back to develop an understanding of where they've been and what they've learned along the way. Before we discuss the tools, let's look at why there is such value in reflecting on and learning from the past.

The role of reflection in career conversations

Academics have spent decades exploring the potential benefits of reflection. As Claude Monet remarked, 'It's on the strength of observation and reflection that one finds a way. So, we must delve unceasingly.'[15] His quote illuminates the importance of learning by reflecting on real-time experiences. Helping employees reflect on their past experiences at work provides invaluable insights. They develop an understanding of what is important to them, what they enjoy and any lessons they have learned.

In his 1985 book *Reflection: Turning Experience Into Learning*, David Boud states, 'Reflection is a generic term for those intellectual and affective activities in which individuals engage to explore their experiences, in order to lead to a new understanding and appreciation.'[16] Thinking about what has happened is part of being human, but casual thinking is different to reflection because it requires a conscious effort. It involves a person considering their experiences in a critical and reflective way to learn and develop insights. This allows them to take meaning from the experience. By transforming those insights into practical strategies, they improve and develop.

---

15   C Moet, *Monet by Himself: Paintings, Drawings, Pastels, Letters* (ed. Chartwell, 2014), https://libquotes.com/claude-monet
16   D Boud, *Reflection: Turning Experience Into Learning* (Routledge, 1985)

Why is reflection important?

Employees will be less able to evaluate or create new opportunities if they don't understand how they reacted to past opportunities. Reflection is about helping employees question, in a positive way, what their experience of work has been like in the past. It is about helping them think about why it has progressed the way it has and the strategies they have used to develop their careers. It is also about the decisions they have made and what they have learned along the way. They can then decide how best to develop their career in the future.

Research has shown that self-reflection can help leaders reach their true potential. Not only does it allow us to consider how we might act differently in the future, but it also increases confidence, self-awareness, empowerment and other positive emotions.[17] Reflection might also strengthen the relationship between employees and their managers or mentors.

It is valuable to help employees reflect both on their successes and their less positive experiences. Almost everyone has experienced a less than 100% positive work experience at one time or another in their work lives. By thinking about what did or didn't go so well, we can help employees identify their strengths and

---

17 JR Bailey & S Rehman, 'Don't Underestimate the Power of Self-Reflection' (*HBR*, 04 March 2022), https://hbr.org/2022/03/dont-underestimate-the-power-of-self-reflection, accessed 23 March 2023

areas for development. Having said that, it's important in those situations to ensure employees don't dwell on the negatives. Helping them to focus on the positives instead teaches them what works well in specific situations. It allows them to examine how they might transfer those strategies to developing their career in the future.

Thinking about an experience is essentially a cognitive activity. Reflection is also emotional and physical and linked with a person's values and social identity. Helping employees view their careers from different perspectives challenges their assumptions and behaviours. It encourages them to see their role differently. It can help them come up with new ideas and options for developing their careers. Reflection also helps employees critically evaluate their working environment. This can help them understand how they might 'fit' within different teams and departments.

How to help employees reflect on their careers

In his book *Learning by Doing: A guide to teaching and learning methods*, academic researcher Graham Gibbs presents his model for effective reflection.[18] Known as Gibbs' Reflective Cycle, the model breaks down the process of reflection into six meaningful and manageable steps. The steps are a useful roadmap for

---

18   G Gibbs, *Learning by Doing: A guide to teaching and learning methods* (Oxford Polytechnic, 1988)

accomplishing reflection using any form of expression (eg, writing, speaking, art):

Step 1: Description. What happened? Ask the employee to share a brief description of the part of their career you are reflecting on. It might be a particular timeframe, a particular role or a significant change or event. Encourage the employee to use the process of telling the story to re-experience it emotionally as well as intellectually.

Step 2: Feelings. What were you thinking and feeling? Ask the employee to describe their thoughts and feelings during this time.

Step 3: Evaluation. What was good or bad about the experience? This step begins the critical thinking involved in meaningful reflection. Ask the employee what they see as the good or bad aspects of the experience now that they are removed from the heat of the moment.

Step 4: Analysis. What sense can they make from the situation? In this step, go beyond the experience and help the employee try to make sense of what happened in the context of other relevant events in their life. Use information available from other experiences to make connections. Use the analysis to generate insights. Areas to consider are their strengths and weaknesses; the aspects of their role that come easily to them, as well as those they find challenging;

the responsibilities they enjoy and don't enjoy; what motivates and drives them; their values and any other considerations that are important to them.

Step 5: Conclusion. What else could they have done? This step builds on the analysis and prepares the employee to integrate the lessons learned from the reflection.

Step 6: Action plan. If the situation arose again, what would you do? Now that they've reflected, help them incorporate what they've learned. For instance, is there anything that they could do or say now to change the outcome? Are there any actions that they can take to prepare for a similar situation in the future? They may also think of other behaviours they can try in similar situations in the future.

You can apply Gibbs' cycle in a variety of ways. Individuals can just think through the different stages, but there is great value in processing thoughts by putting them into language – either written or spoken. The most obvious way to help employees reflect is in one-to-one conversations with the manager asking employees questions. You might also provide employees with questions to consider and respond to in advance. Writing their answers will help them prepare for a reflective discussion. You can even encourage reflection in a visual format.

A final word of warning. Reflection doesn't need rules or much time, but it is one of the easiest tasks to drop when the pressure is on. Try to remember that this is one of the most valuable tools to help employees focus on the areas of their work that really matter to them.

When people think about careers, they are often so focused on the future that they forget all the rich learning they can get from the past. The following three tools will help employees with that reflection.

#1 Career Platform tool: Where are they starting from?

This is a tool that you can use to quickly help an employee determine what they want to change in their career and motivate them to act. *Career Platform* is a tool that helps establish the starting point for this part of their career journey. It's about recognising that they've already come some way on the journey and then helping them get clear on what they do and don't want to change. In other words, it's about establishing a solid platform to kick off from rather than thinking they're starting from scratch. It's also about identifying who and what is important to them in making this journey and what support they want from you in thinking it through.

Career Platform questions

Sometimes, employees want something to be different, but they believe it's up to someone else (their manager, HR or the organisation) to create the change. The questions are deliberately worded in a way that frames the conversation as a positive, solution-focused one. Typical *Career Platform* questions are:

- What is going well in your current role?

- What would you not want to change?

- What would you like to be different?

- What would be the benefit of that?

- Who else would that affect?

These last questions are important. For people to change, they need to see that making that change will result in a personal benefit. They need to know what's in it for them – especially as changing their behaviour can be difficult and challenging.

The insight could be that learning a new skill (which demands energy and effort) will result in them changing the way they manage their team. This will provide them with more time and less stress: a clear personal benefit. It might be even more personal than that. Start with exploring the benefits to them personally and then move on to others – their bosses, their team, their peers and even their family.

CAREER PLATFORM IN PRACTICE

Tracey was a senior HR Manager in a university.
Her boss was the HR Director and in our first meeting,
the manager said, 'Tracey is a valuable member of my
team. She is a good project leader and knowledgeable
about the university. She's also skilled at developing
relationships and working at a senior level. However,
a couple of things haven't gone well in the past
few months and I'm afraid these have affected her
confidence and resilience. She seems to be struggling
with managing her workload and isn't showing as much
promise as she used to.'

Tracey and I went into a private meeting room to get
to know each other better and once we were on our
own, her face crumpled and she started crying. She
said, 'I'm so unhappy. I used to love my job, but I feel
like I've lost my way and don't know how to find my way
back.' Gently, I started asking her the *Career Platform*
questions. When I asked her about what was going well
and what she would not want to change, she said, 'Most
of the job is going OK. I love the people I work with
and I really enjoy managing projects and working with
senior leaders. I just feel like I can't get everything done.
I'm missing deadlines and I'm worried that I'm letting
people down.'

I could see that Tracey was in danger of spiralling into
negativity and despair. I said, 'I can see that this is really
taking a toll on you and causing you a lot of stress
and anxiety. What would you like to be different?' She
replied, 'I just want to feel more in control. I'd like to get
some clarity over my career direction and my options. I'd
like to enjoy coming to work more.' When I asked who

else that would affect and what the benefit would be, she became quite animated. She said the main person who would notice would be her husband, because she went home every night and moaned about what she saw as her failings. She said, 'He's very supportive, but I can tell he's getting frustrated by my lack of self-confidence.' She also thought her team would notice. She had short hair, and it was a bit of a joke in the team that when she got stressed, she had 'high hair' because she was always running her hands through it.

That conversation and that reflection helped Tracey realise that developing her career wasn't just about her, and it wasn't just about her manager and what her manager thought about her. It was about her whole life – not just work, but home as well. The impact it was having on her marriage and her team really spurred her on. She sat up straight, looked me in the eye and her whole demeanour and body language said, 'OK. Here we go. I'm going to do something about this.' That wasn't even our first session, it was just the pre-meeting. Just by thinking through who was affected, and how, she was motivated to do something about it and even identified some small steps she could take immediately.

Tips for using the Career Platform tool

- The *Career Platform* can be quite general – the specifics often come later.

- By nature, people tend to start from a position of what they want to change and what they're not happy about. Acknowledge that and be empathetic, but don't get drawn into discussing the negatives.

- Explore how willing the individual is to take ownership of influencing what they can about the situation. Encourage them to think about the benefits of that to themselves, but also to others who may be affected.

#2 Your Journey So Far tool: How did they get here?

The second tool that focuses on the past is the *Your Journey So Far* tool. *Your Journey So Far* is a tool that encourages employees to reflect on their career to date. You might encourage them to reflect on their whole career, or a certain role or a certain time period, whichever is most appropriate. The tool is designed to help them reflect on what they're good at, what's most important to them, what keeps them engaged and how they like to work.

💬 Your Journey So Far questions

Typical questions to help employees look back over their career are:

- What are you most proud of?
- What is it about that achievement that you found satisfying?

- When was your most enjoyable time at work?

- What did you enjoy most about that time?

- What helped you get where you are today?

These questions are deliberately worded to encourage employees to share stories describing themselves as resourceful, capable and able to deal with challenges rather than someone who has drifted through their career never achieving anything. Even though employees will have faced several challenges during their career, the focus is on what helped them overcome those challenges and cope with difficulties.

YOUR JOURNEY SO FAR IN PRACTICE

Matthew worked as a Head of IT for the NHS and he was facing a reorganisation. There was going to be a reduction in staff and it was possible that the Newcastle office where he was based was going to close. He was a lovely man, very gentle with a warm smile and kind eyes. He reminded me of John Candy in *Planes, Trains and Automobiles*. He was in his late fifties, and he said to me, 'People keep asking me if I'm going to retire, but I don't want to retire. I want to position myself so I'm in the best place to get a role in the future.' The thing he really wanted help with was to develop the confidence to go for a job at a higher level and to develop greater belief in his own abilities.

When we explored *Your Journey So Far*, I was flabbergasted. This lovely, modest man regaled a story of running his own business, managing the closure of one of the divisions of a company he worked for, turning around a failed department and being a rally driver. What became abundantly clear was that this was a man who thrived on challenge and competition. He was always looking at new ways to build, create and improve. What had helped him get where he was today was driving change, solving complex problems and pushing the system to a higher level. What also became clear was that he was seen as a 'safe pair of hands' because his current role was about maintaining the systems and protecting the status quo. He realised he needed to share the stories of his experience and achievements before and outside of his current role so people saw him as the change agent that he was and wanted to continue being.

Tips for using the Your Journey So Far tool

- Be flexible. You can look at different periods of time. You can look at a specific role or a specific project. You can look at a person's work life or you can take a broader view and also encompass life outside work.

- Listen for the themes in what they found most enjoyable and satisfying.

- Identify their underlying drivers, motivators and values.

- Encourage them to reflect on the specific actions they took to make progress.

- Reflect on the positive skills, qualities and resources they have shown.

#3 Career Kitbag tool: What resources do they have?

The third of our tools that focuses on the past is the *Career Kitbag* tool. Most people are disconnected from the resources they have at their disposal but strongly drawn to what's missing. In other words, they can be very aware of their areas for development, but have lost sight of their skills, strengths and talents. Employees need help identifying and focusing on all the resources they have that will help them make progress. That's what is in their Career Kitbag. Those resources are their experiences, their skills, their positive qualities, their unique talents and their contribution that sets them apart from others. As a manager or as a mentor, this is a great opportunity for you to feed back to them what strengths you can see in them that perhaps they have lost sight of or weren't aware of in themselves. This is where you can remind them of all the success stories you've heard, as well as the positive skills, qualities, behaviours and attitudes that you've observed.

💬 Career Kitbag questions

Questions that help you identify their resources are:

- What useful experiences have helped you get where you are today?

- What valuable skills have you developed?

- What positive qualities will help you make progress?

- What unique talents do you have that will help?

- What contribution do you make to your team and organisation that sets you apart from others?

These questions help employees identify a wealth of resources. Not all of them might be immediately useful in further developing their career, but identifying them helps employees remain constructive and resilient in the face of change and uncertainty. Examining how they have successfully tackled career challenges in the past is a great way of unearthing strengths. By examining how they have risen to a challenge, you can pinpoint a wealth of useful ideas and resources that they can deploy now or later.

CAREER KITBAG IN PRACTICE

Linda was coming to the end of her assignment in the NHS. She wanted to develop a clearer understanding of her knowledge and skills and an idea of where she wanted to get to so she could evaluate the opportunities offered to her. She was a lovely lady, full of energy and spark and very conversational. She had three children, aged ten, six and four and worked part-time as a project manager. It quickly became clear that, despite being obviously intelligent, capable and very talented, she didn't recognise that. The way she put it was, 'I feel like a china dog. Very nice, but what's it for?' We spent a few sessions working through each of the different *Career*

Kitbag questions and gradually built up her *Career Kitbag*. Her skills were in project management, taking ideas from initiation to completion and developing innovative approaches and solutions. In particular, she was brilliant at making connections and joining up the best practice that existed in different parts of the organisation. She became really clear on her skills, strengths and preferred role. We found a way for her to articulate that in a couple of sentences. She was later offered a role as a Network Delivery Manager, which was a perfect fit for her skills.

Tips for using the Career Kitbag tool

- Encourage them to identify all the resources they already have that will help them make progress.

- Knowledge, experience and relationships are all valuable resources, as well as personal qualities and personality attributes.

- Skills include technical skills, people skills, leadership skills, business skills and career development skills.

- Provide genuine, positive feedback based on what you know and have observed.

Those are the three tools that help people learn from the past. What I'd really like you to do now is put them into practice by having a career conversation with someone using these three tools. It might not be an employee. At this stage, you may wish to try out the questions with a friend or family member.

8
Dreaming About
The Future

I n this chapter, we're going to look at the Career Conversation tools that focus on the future. In other words, where people are going. Those are the *Future Success* tool, the *Career Routes* tool and the *Career Kitbag Additions* tool. The fundamental principle underlying this set of tools is that career development is a journey, not a destination. These tools help determine a general direction and the variety of options and routes to get there. First though, let's take a look at a powerful technique that acts as the bridge between where someone is in their career at any given moment to where they want to be.

Harnessing the power of visualisation in career conversations

You want your employees to be successful, don't you? In fact, you and they have probably used that word. Do you know what success really means to them? Have they truly thought about it and discussed it with you? People talk about success all the time, but they rarely define it in a way that is meaningful to them and can be shared with others. That's where visualisation can help, but it's not as easy as asking employees to visualise the success they want and expecting it to happen. Visualisation can be used as a practical tool with employees to help them take ownership of their career development.

Visualisation is the ability for someone to create a clear picture in their mind of the exact work experience and circumstance they wish to create. It is seeing, feeling and completely embodying a future outcome – whether that's getting promoted, working in a different role or reducing their hours – before it happens. By creating a picture of their desired future success in their mind in as much detail as possible, they can create the energy and enthusiasm to move towards it. Think about building a jigsaw puzzle. Have you ever attempted to build one without having the box top to look at? It is extremely difficult to complete the puzzle without knowing what the outcome looks like. You may fit pieces together. You may get bits and pieces of the puzzle done, but it will take longer, be more challenging and possibly never reach completion. The same is true of a person's career: the clearer and more detailed someone is when they visualise what they want from their career, the easier it will be to make it a reality.

That may sound simplistic and optimistic, but it's backed up by neuroscience. Research has shown that the brain doesn't distinguish between whether something is real or whether we just imagine it as real. The famous 'piano study'[19] is an excellent example. Researchers at Harvard University, led by Alvaro Pascual-Leone, compared the brains of people playing a sequence of notes on the piano with the brains of people imagining playing the notes. The region of the brain connected to the finger muscles was found to have changed to the same degree in both groups of people, regardless of whether they struck the keys physically or mentally.

It is the fact that the brain processes imaginary events as if they are real that allows sports people to benefit from visualisation. Almost every elite athlete does mental practice as well as physical practice. They visualise themselves carrying out their sport and doing everything right in exact detail. This means their brain learns this way of operating and ensures their body learns to work in the way they're imagining.

---

19 A Pascual-Leone, *The Brain That Plays Music and Is Changed By It* (*Annals of the New York Academy of Sciences*, June 2001), https://pubmed.ncbi.nlm.nih.gov/11458838, accessed 27 March 2023

The same phenomenon allows us to benefit from the power of visualisation in career development. Visualisation acts as the bridge between where someone is in their career at any given moment to where they want to be – by allowing them to see and feel their future success as if it has happened.

My personal experience of visualisation is that it is highly powerful for a few different reasons:

1. **It focuses an employee's attention.** One of the problems many people face with career development is that they are so busy with day-to-day tasks that they don't think about the future. Visualisation helps employees focus on what they want. When they're focused, they spot opportunities to move towards their future success. It's what I call the 'serendipity factor'. They're more likely to be in the right place at the right time.

2. **It helps them progress and take action.** As explained above, when an employee visualises, their brain processes it as if it is happening now. And because their brain thinks their desired future success has already happened, they're more likely to take the actions necessary to align with their brain's perceived reality.

3. **It makes employees feel empowered.** When employees visualise their future success, it brings them a sense of empowerment. They

start to notice small changes in their work life as they move in the direction they want to go. This brings them a belief in themselves and what they are doing. They start to realise that there is a lot they can do to make progress.

The key to visualisation is to encourage employees to be as specific as possible. As you listen to their description, build up a picture in your mind. Help them to focus on all the small details, from what they're wearing, to what they're doing, to what they're saying. For example, if they would like to be promoted, visualise what that looks like. What do they wake up to in the morning? How do they commute? What do they wear? What does their desk look like? What do they hear in the conversations around them? Help to draw out the visualisation by asking questions. If they want to move into a leadership role, you might respond with, 'Tell me about your first challenge in a leadership role. What's the first thing you want to achieve? Who do you have with you to make it happen?' There's something very powerful about helping an employee talk through their vision. Not only does talking about it build their commitment to making it happen, but it also helps them flesh out the vision. Making it increasingly detailed makes it much more real.

Of course, while visualisation can help energise and motivate employees, for real progress, it needs to be paired with action. That's what the next three Career Conversation tools are designed to help with.

#4 Future Success tool: What does success mean to them?

The *Future Success* tool is the key tool to help people visualise and think creatively about their future success. It helps them think about their future and opens up possibilities.

Before we get to the questions in the *Future Success* tool, I'd like to talk a little about the concept of 'success'. Success means different things to different people. Everyone's definition will be personal to them. Success doesn't have to mean moving up in an organisation, taking on more responsibility or managing more people and a bigger budget. When I talk about *Future Success*, people sometimes think I mean career goals or objectives. I don't. In fact, I think career goals and objectives can be quite limiting. That is especially true if people use the SMART model developed for managing performance. SMART is an acronym that stands for Specific, Measurable, Attainable, Results-focused and Timebound. When people try and be SMART with their career development, they constrain themselves by describing success by position or job title. In other words, they define their career goal along the lines of, 'I want to be a (job title) by (date),' or, 'I want to be promoted to a (grade) by (date).' These goals are SMART in so much as they are Specific, Measurable, Attainable, Results-focused and Timebound, but they are not particularly helpful because they limit options and possibilities.

The original purpose of SMART goals was to manage projects and performance. They assume a predictability and a degree of influence and control. The way to make progress is to set a goal and then create a plan to work towards it. Does that scenario really apply when managing your career (especially in an ever-changing organisation operating in an emergent, surprising world)? The key to using the *Future Success* tool is to get beyond the simplicity and constraints created by a 'job' or a 'job title'. Instead, it is about getting employees to describe in detail how life will be when they have achieved their ambitions, which opens up all sorts of possibilities. At this stage, it doesn't matter if it is realistic or not. After all, do we ever really achieve our ambitions? They're always changing and evolving. They are like the horizon. They serve as a valuable guide and a direction, but as you make progress towards them, they continue to move ahead of you. The purpose of the discussion is simply to fix career direction so employees can explore the many ways to get to their destination. The choices available to them may include a change in role upwards or sidewards, but the greatest opportunities come from finding ways to help them develop in their current role.

💬 Future Success questions

One way you can help employees think about their future is to ask them to imagine that a miracle happens. For example: Suppose you could wave a magic wand and develop your career in exactly the way you'd like...

- What would you be doing day to day?

- Where would you be working?

- What kind of people would you be working with/for?

- What would you be delivering or producing and who for?

- Why is that important to you?

With each question, allow them lots of space to answer. There are no right or wrong answers. They can be as creative and as imaginative as they like if it's something they would enjoy. Be curious. Ask whatever questions you need to build up a picture in your head of what they're describing.

FUTURE SUCCESS IN PRACTICE

Mark was a Client Services Director for an advertising agency. He had two people who both said they wanted to be account managers, but there was only one account manager role and it was already filled. I encouraged him to use the *Future Success* tool with each team member to explore what they were really hoping for.

DREAMING ABOUT THE FUTURE

The next time we met, I asked him how he'd got on. He said, 'One team member, Kate, talked about working more with clients. She wants to manage the team responsible for developing the whole ad campaign. She saw herself chairing meetings with the client and leading on client presentations. She also wants to be doing more to develop the agency and how it's run. She's ambitious and she wants the challenge that comes with new roles and responsibilities.' Mark went on to say, 'That's great, because I can give her opportunities to do all of those things to a greater or lesser extent in her current role.' He started taking Kate to client presentations with him and giving her small projects that went through the whole ad life cycle so that she could see more of the whole picture and learn from it. Mark had too much to do, so involving her more helped them both. When the account manager role became available, Kate was in a much better position to apply for it. Not only had she demonstrated her commitment to the organisation, but she was also clear on what the role involved and what would be needed to take on the new responsibilities. She had been given the opportunity to test out her aspirations and was even more certain that she wanted the challenge that came with the position.

What about the other team member? 'Sam said she wanted more money,' said Mark. 'There's nothing much I can do about that. She's considering taking a year off to go travelling.' Sure enough, Sam did leave shortly afterwards. In this scenario, Mark was able to satisfy the aspirations of one individual and not the other.

That will sometimes be the case. You can't always make everybody happy, but in connecting the needs of the people to the needs of the organisation, Mark was able to satisfy the aspirations of the person that was committed to the organisation and for whom the organisation was a good fit. That's important. We have to think about the organisational considerations as well as the individuals.

👥 Tips for using the Future Success tool

- Listen carefully and give plenty of space.

- This is a creative process and needs time for thinking and reflection so don't rush it.

- Look for details and signs of what is wanted, not what isn't. If necessary, turn it around with, 'And what would you be doing instead?'

- Look for small visible details expressed in simple words.

- Build up a picture. If you can't see it in your mind's eye then you need more specifics.

- Use, 'What else?' to get lots of different detail and build up the description.

- This is all about what it's like when success has been achieved – not how to get there. That comes later.

#5 Career Routes tool: What are the options and possibilities?

Our next tool that focuses on the future is the *Career Routes* tool. This tool recognises that there are many ways to get to a destination. You can take the direct route, the indirect route, the fast way or the slow way.

When helping people explore their options and possibilities, it's important to highlight that the number one skill required for someone to develop their career is influence. There are three different spheres of influence that employees need to be aware of. The first sphere is the employees' attitude and behaviour in their current role, which is something they can affect directly. The second sphere involves influencing their manager to broaden their role by giving them new opportunities, projects, responsibilities or assignments. The third sphere involves influencing beyond the manager to secure a new role. This needs the buy-in of others or a process to be carried out.

In his famous book, *7 Habits of Highly Effective People*,[20] Stephen Covey introduced the concept of a smaller Circle of Influence within a larger Circle of Concern. The Circle of Concern comprises all matters about which a person cares. The Circle of Influence includes those matters that a person can affect directly.

---

20 S Covey, *7 Habits of Highly Effective People* (Simon & Schuster UK, 21 November 2013)

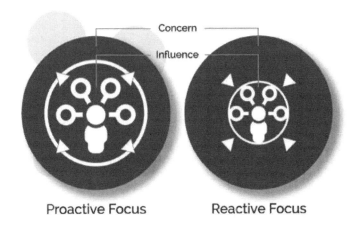

Proactive Focus   Reactive Focus

Expanding your Circle of Influence. Adapted from S Covey,
7 Habits of Highly Effective People (Simon & Schuster, 1989)

He explains that the Circle of Influence is like a muscle that enlarges and gains elasticity with exercise, but wastes away with lack of use. When people focus on elements they can influence (eg, their relationships with others, their personal productivity), they expand their knowledge and experience and they build trustworthiness. As a result, their Circle of Influence grows. However, when people focus on aspects they can't control, they have less time and energy to spend on aspects they can influence. Consequently, their Circle of Influence shrinks.

The three spheres of influence in career development work in a similar way. When employees focus on their attitude and behaviour in their current role, they improve their performance and productivity. That enhances their value in the eyes of their manager, who will then provide them with new opportunities and increased responsibilities. That, in turn, will enhance their reputation in the organisation, making it easier to influence people and processes outside their current role and manager. The role of managers is to help employees focus on their attitude and behaviour in their current role first and then work with them to broaden their role in a way that meets their needs as well as adding value to the organisation. This will broaden their options of new roles if that is their desire.

People still move upwards in a career. In some instances, people get promoted into more senior roles within their organisations. In other instances, people move to take on more senior roles in other organisations. Up is still an option, but it's not the only way. It was never the only way, or the best way, or even the most satisfying way to navigate a career, but for many years it was the accepted image of career progression.

Career progression is specific to everyone. It is about how they improve their enjoyability and employability. Those two areas will be different for everyone depending on how much they want to grow, stretch, learn and transform. Here are six different kinds of career journeys. How those might contribute to a person's personal progression is up to them to decide:

1. Continuing on the same path. A person can continue along the same path and make a current role more interesting and challenging. They might get rid of some tasks and take on others. A small shift can transform their current job into a more exciting opportunity to learn new skills. Specialists build entire careers from continuing the same path. They continually improve at what they do and deepen their contribution along the way. Ask yourself what you learned this week or this month. You might be surprised. This is the route I have taken since starting my business ten years ago. My job title remains unchanged, but my role has evolved as the business has evolved. I continue to focus on improving my performance and developing new skills. I can assure you, I am *never* bored!

2. Finding out the route others have taken. Finding out the route others have taken gives a person the opportunity to explore possibilities for their own career development journey. It may involve short-term work assignments or shadowing someone who is in a position they may be considering. The exploratory experience could be as simple as having a conversation about the requirements of a role that seems attractive. It's a chance to check out a role to see what will work – and what might *not* work. Exploring is smart step to take before investing time and energy in pursuing other routes. Ask employees to think about an assignment that intrigues them. How could they learn more about it?

This is what I did at the start of my career. About four years after graduating, I realised I was not excited about developing washing powders (I was a Technical Brand Manager for P&G). I had started getting involved in corporate training and found that much more interesting. My mentor helped me secure an opportunity to deliver training to PhD students as part of the company's graduate recruitment efforts. It was a great way to test out a new role before making the move.

3. Reversing or braking. People sometimes choose to pause their career development journey or reverse to refocus. Maybe the current role was just not a fit and they're brave enough to admit it. Maybe this step opens a whole new vista that seems exciting in a part of the organisation that's new or growing. It can also be about finding a role that is less demanding, more enjoyable and better aligned with personal priorities. With the ever-increasing focus on work/life balance, a reverse move is sometimes based on a personal need that, if ignored, might result in resignation and exit. Reversing usually means letting go of certain responsibilities, time commitments and, potentially, salary. Whatever the reason, it's a valid, important option.

This is the route I took when I made the decision to leave my role in product research for P&G and take up a role in training and development. I moved to a new organisation and started again. I took a pay cut, but it was worth it and I've never looked back.

4. Moving sideways. Moving sideways refers to broadening a person's role by taking on extra challenges or responsibilities. It might also involve a new role where status and scope of responsibility are typically the same or similar. A new perspective is the payoff from moving sideways. Employees get to see a different part of the landscape. When someone takes on a role in another function or department, they get to view their responsibilities and the organisation through a new lens. By moving sideways, people can fine-tune their skills, build new relationships and learn a new or different approach. They can get deeper hands-on expertise, see the organisational operations from a different angle and add to their knowledge base. What sideways options could offer a new view?

My most significant sideways move was when I moved from a training role in Accenture to a training role in Avanade. The status and scope of responsibility were similar, but Avanade was a startup with very different challenges to Accenture. It opened my eyes and remains one of the most defining moments of my career.

5. Taking the uphill option. As I've said, the ladder hasn't completely disappeared. The rungs aren't all gone. For some people, a move up makes absolute sense. When it works for the organisation and the individual, a vertical move can be included in the journey. Vertical moves can bring with them many of the traditional symbols of success like titles and monetary compensation. A vertical experience could mean leading a team or project and taking on a more visible role. They can also come with headaches, so careful thought about when, if and how a vertical move would fit into a person's career experience is essential. How will they know when or if a vertical move is right?

I have made many vertical moves in my career. Some were positive, rewarding and exciting. Some were less so.

6. Starting a new journey. People don't always have to continue the same journey. Starting a new journey means leaving for an entirely new organisation or industry. It's awkward and sometimes tough to acknowledge this one. However, it is real and every person knows the option to start a new journey is there. In the past, once you started a new journey, there was no opportunity to return. Today, it's exciting to see how many who leave an organisation are welcomed back when they decide to return. One good reason is they bring a wealth of new knowledge with them.

I started a new journey when I left corporate life and set up my own business. Starting a new journey is a strong option if you have a strong desire to be an entrepreneur. It might be the right option if someone can find job satisfaction *only* in roles that are not available in the organisation.

I have shared six different possible career routes to consider. As you have read, I have taken them all at one time or another. Ultimately, the selection of the different experiences is down to the individual.

Everyone's career journey is unique but one thing is true for everybody. Taking a broad and flexible approach to growth is key in this fast-changing world. Adopting a mindset that views change as an opportunity can open new landscapes for development.

💬 Career Routes questions

Questions to explore the different options and possibilities include:

- How might you make your current role more satisfying and enjoyable?

- How might you broaden your role?

- How might you gain specific skills and experience through special projects, responsibilities or assignments?

- How might you gain greater visibility, responsibility and challenge?

- How might you explore different possibilities and alternatives?

CAREER ROUTES IN PRACTICE

Sophie was anxious that she wasn't realising her full potential. She felt she'd drifted into her current role after university and wondered whether to stay where she was or move to something different. As a project manager, she was moving between different projects and different functions and felt very much that she was responding to others' demands rather than driving her own career. She wanted to feel confident about taking the next step in her career and that it would be achievable. When she defined her future success, it transpired that the content of the job was less important to her than her work environment, which was currently challenging because of some difficult colleagues. The most important elements were flexible work patterns, autonomy in carrying out the work, living near her family, being intellectually challenged and her relationships with her work colleagues. Her strengths were in project management, getting work done and her interpersonal sensitivity, which meant she was good at influencing without authority. She realised she wasn't particularly concerned about climbing the organisation's hierarchy. Once we had defined these criteria, plus others, it became clear that there were lots of different options and possibilities. She could stay in her current role and try and deal with some of the relationship challenges. She could move to a different function within the same organisation to get more challenge and stimulation, as well as a better work environment. Or, she could move to a new organisation that might have a better culture. In the end, she chose the second option and was much happier as a result.

👥 Tips for using the Career Routes tool

- Career Routes range from options that are totally within the employee's influence (their own attitude and behaviour in their current role), to options that need the support of the manager (broadening the current role or identifying special projects and assignments), to options that need the support of the organisation (moving role or getting promoted). The greatest opportunities come from identifying development in the current role.

- Focus first on the current role and explore ways to make it more enjoyable and satisfying.

- Then, focus on how the current role could be broadened to provide new opportunities.

- Finally, explore opportunities outside the current role.

#6 Career Kitbag Additions tool: What do they need to make progress?

Once we have identified the different options that are available, we can go on to analyse what resources the individual will need to make progress. That brings us to the *Career Kitbag Additions* tool.

We need to remind people of all the resources they already have in their *Career Kitbag*, but we mustn't lose sight of the additional resources they may need. This tool allows you to help people generate a broad pool of skills, experiences, information and relationships that they will need to make progress. Before we get into the specifics of the tool, I'd like to explore the types of skills and capabilities employees need to succeed in the changing workplace.

As I outlined in Chapter 1, there are five major trends that will impact on the future of work and career development: technology, changing demographics, the global pandemic, globalisation and business shift. According to a World Economic Forum report, it's expected that, 'by 2025, 85 million jobs may be displaced by a shift in the division of labour between humans and machines'.[21] They will be replaced by new and exciting jobs to fit around our fast-developing technology. At the same time, our world faces new problems to be solved (the most recent and obvious being the global pandemic).

While employees may not be able to future-proof their jobs, they can future-proof their careers. Encourage them to have an open mind about what the change may bring. Emphasise that change is an opportunity for growth rather than a need to fear a shift in status quo. When organisations adopt new technologies and automations, they free employees to perform other, more value-adding work. This is a great opportunity for individuals to shine, provided they're ready to take more responsibility for their careers and are working to future-proof them. Their ability to be flexible and take full advantage of change will be the difference between being left behind and using it as an opportunity to develop and progress.

---

21 WEF, 'The Future of Jobs Report 2020', World Economic Forum (October 2020), www3.weforum.org/docs/WEF_Future_of_Jobs_2020.pdf, accessed 27 March 2023

Understanding the future of the industry or sector

Understanding the future of your industry or sector is a major factor in future-proofing someone's career. Everything that happens in the industry as a whole will likely impact the organisation they work for, as well as their role within it. Explore with employees how they can follow changes and trends in the profession, the industry, and the wider economy to keep informed. They can keep up to date by reading quality news and industry publications. Consider the political, economic, social and technological changes shaping the environment.

One key strategy to future-proofing someone's career is to try to anticipate which technologies the organisation is likely to adopt. There are several ways to do that. They can observe technology trends in the industry and they can also pay attention to what leaders are saying about the company's goals for digital transformation. For example, there's a good chance that artificial intelligence (AI) solutions are coming to the organisation soon. Since future-proofing their career means being able to work with AI, they'll need to be fluent in those technologies.

Developing new skills

As the working world becomes increasingly powered by digital, there is a high probability that employees will need new technological skills to succeed. Many industries are already relying on tech to streamline and automate their processes, so a technical skillset is critical. Employees need to expand on this skillset to remain relevant, but they shouldn't just focus on growing and refining their technical abilities. Robots may be able to automate the technical skills of a job, but soft skills such as leadership, communication and collaboration are still tasks that only humans do well. Since robots do not have the same emotional intelligence as humans, these soft skills are, and will continue to be, in high demand. The introduction of new technologies in the workplace is likely to drive up demand for the following soft skills:

1. Complex problem-solving (ie, solving problems that have no clear or 'right' answer): Complex problem-solving is a soft skill required by every job. This skill uses both logic and creativity. People need to be able to apply reason to solve problems, but creativity is also necessary for coming up with a solution.

2. Creativity (ie, the use of imagination or original ideas to create something): The main thing about creativity is that it is unique to every individual. Every person is capable of being creative – it isn't limited to just being good at painting. Thinking creatively is a soft skill valued by many employers. It means you can 'think outside the box' and contribute fresh new ideas to the organisation.

3. Collaboration (ie, working well with others): Being able to work with other people who might be from a variety of different backgrounds is an important skill to have. Nearly every job involves some level of working collaboratively or as part of a team.

4. Critical thinking (ie, being able to analyse and test something and form a judgement about it): Critical thinking is all about analysis and organisations value individuals with this skill. It is the key to making improvements. If we all took everything at face value, nothing would ever be improved. It is the skill of critical thinking that helps to lead employees to make contributions.

5. Emotional intelligence (ie, being aware of your own, and others', emotions): Being emotionally intelligent at work is a vital skill that organisations look for. Roles involving customer service or interaction need a great deal of emotional intelligence. Working in an environment with other colleagues also requires a sensitivity to others. To keep up morale and productivity, it is important that people are aware of each other's emotions.

6. Self-awareness (ie, knowing yourself, your strengths, weaknesses, emotions and behaviour): Being self-aware is a necessary life-skill that can be applied to all jobs. It is vital to be aware of your own strengths and weaknesses, as well as

the effect you have on others. Self-awareness at work is essential for helping with productivity and relationships.

7. Curiosity (ie, having a learning mindset and always asking 'why'): Curiosity is the partner of critical thinking. Questioning why things happen in the way they do is the first step to making improvements. This is especially valuable for developing new systems and policies.

8. Resilience (ie, picking yourself up and moving on from problems, hurdles and negativity): Resilience will have as much a place in the future of work as it does in the present. All jobs involve problem-solving, and when things go wrong, it is important that people can move forward and learn from these experiences.

9. Adaptability (ie, finding ways around a problem, being comfortable with change and adapting): Adaptability is the number one power skill to future-proof careers. With so much change being foreseen in the future of work, employees will have to be ready to cope with anything the future throws at them. To be adaptable, they need to have an open mind, be able to cope with change and pick up new skills quickly. It means being responsive to their environment. It is highly valuable in the workplace as it means that whatever skills they don't already have, they will be capable of learning them.

Building their professional network

It is important for employees to take time to develop relationships with people within and outside of the organisation. These people can be invaluable support as the landscape of work changes. Employees can learn tips and tricks from inspiring leaders, as well as boost their exposure for new opportunities.

If networking is something they're not over-familiar with, LinkedIn is a great starting point. Encourage employees to join professional groups, access training webinars and check in with former colleagues. Other ways to build their network include joining online forums and professional associations. They can also take part in industry events and activities. Emphasise that the success of networking relies on quality, not quantity. Adding contacts to a network via LinkedIn and Twitter is an easy way to grow it, but this doesn't tell you how healthy those connections are. It is more important for employees to focus their networking efforts on building relationships with people.

💬 Career Kitbag Additions questions

- What knowledge do you need to gain?
- What skills do you need to develop?
- What experience do you need to get?

- What behaviours and achievements do you need to demonstrate?

- What relationships do you need to develop?

CAREER KITBAG ADDITIONS IN PRACTICE

George was a director in a charity. The CEO had announced that he would be leaving in six months and George had decided he would apply for the position. George had many years of experience in the sector and in the organisation, so he already had a well-stocked Career Kitbag. However, he knew there were things he would have to add to it if he was going to be seen as someone who could step up into the CEO role. As CEO, he would be much more outwardly facing so he needed to build his knowledge of the sector and what other charities in that space were doing. He would need to develop his public speaking skills and get more experience of speaking to the media and government policy-makers. He would need to be seen as someone who could take a tough position against challenge and criticism and, above all, he would need to develop his relationships with the trustees on the board. He developed a plan of meetings with key stakeholders and started taking and creating opportunities to build his profile internally and externally. Unfortunately, he didn't get the job. Politically, there were drivers to bring someone in from outside, but his preparation was hugely valuable, nonetheless. He impressed the new CEO with his knowledge and relationships and played a critical role in helping the CEO transition into the organisation. When a CEO role came up within the sector, he was well positioned and he successfully applied for the position.

 Tips for using the Career Kitbag Additions tool

- Analyse the Future Success and different career routes to determine new resources that will be needed.

- Identify the decision-makers that will need to be influenced.

- Explore what they will need to see and hear to be supportive.

So, those are our three tools that help people dream about the future: the *Future Success* tool, the *Career Routes* tool and the *Career Kitbag Additions* tool.

9

Career Conversation Tools Focused On The Present

In this chapter, we're going to look at the Career Conversation tools that focus on the present. Those are the *Career Checkpoint* tool, the *Short-Term Milestones* tool and the *Setting Off* tool. We're also going to look at the final tool in the toolkit, the *Progress Review* tool. These tools are designed according to the principle that career development is about helping people make the most of their career journey.

#7 Career Checkpoint tool: Where are they in relation to where they want to go?

Employees often forget all they appreciate and value about their role, their team and their organisation. The purpose of the *Career Checkpoint* tool is to connect reality to the aspirational destination they described in response to the *Future Success* tool. It allows them to identify all the ways their current role is already satisfying their aspirations and to highlight the progress they have already made.

The *Career Checkpoint* tool uses a simple scale of one to ten, but in a deliberately solution-focused way. We use scales quite regularly in day-to-day language, but as human beings, we are naturally deficit-focused. The phraseology of the *Career Checkpoint* tool turns that on its head. It starts by asking, 'On a scale of one to ten, where ten is your picture of future success, where are you today?' It then goes on to ask, 'What makes your score that high? What's going well?' The questions ask about all the aspects of the role that are working. These help people be more positive and optimistic about where they are now and energised to make progress.

💬 Career Checkpoint questions

On a scale of one to ten, where ten is your picture of Future Success:

- Where are you today?

- What makes your score that high? What's going well?

- What elements of your *Future Success* are already in place?

- When do you get glimpses of your *Future Success* in your current role?

- What progress have you already made?

CAREER CHECKPOINT IN PRACTICE

Grace had been with her organisation all her career. She started in customer service at nineteen years old and had progressed to become one of the sales managers. She managed the three largest accounts for the business, but was frustrated because the only way to win more work from them was to develop new products. It was clear she was starting to feel bored and a bit stale.

When we explored her *Future Success*, she described a picture where she'd moved away from doing the day-to-day sales activity to directing/managing the work. She was seen as the go-to person for new initiatives and she had a clear strategy for winning new business. When we started exploring the *Career Checkpoint* questions, she said she was a four on a scale of one to ten. Her shoulders dropped as she said it and she immediately started explaining why it wasn't higher. I gently interrupted her and said, 'Before we get to that, why don't you tell me why you're at four and not lower.' She said, 'All those things do happen to a varying degree. I've got good relationships with the others in the office; the Sales Director asks my opinion regularly and I've got some good ideas on how we should develop our strategy.' She also described a new initiative that she'd managed to get off the ground by presenting it to the senior management team and getting agreement to use resources from other departments. As she talked, her shoulders lifted and eyes sparkled as she described the new initiative and the challenges she'd overcome to get it off the ground.

As a result of the discussion, she'd realised that there were simple actions she could take to move towards five on the scale. She decided to sketch out the ideas she had about the sales strategy and make an appointment with the Sales Director so she could share them with him and hopefully move them forwards.

 Tips for using the Career Checkpoint tool

Ask, look and listen for:

- What's going well.
- What elements of their Future Success are already in place.
- When they get glimpses of their Future Success in their current role.
- What's helped them make progress.
- Interrupt them if they start telling you why it's not higher and refocus them on the positives.

#8 Short-Term Milestones tool: What is their next checkpoint?

Developing a picture of future success can be inspiring and energising for employees, but if that picture is at ten on the scale and they are only at three or four, it can sometimes have the opposite effect because it seems so far away that it's hardly worth trying. So, in the short term, we encourage employees not to worry about ten, but instead identify a more manageable short-term milestone that will take them in the direction of their future success (or at least help them discover what works and what doesn't). Perhaps they had ideas and assumptions that looked good in theory, but when applied they didn't work out as they had thought. On the other hand, their plans and ideas might expand into opportunities and options that they hadn't imagined before. They might gain more insights into a role or opportunity they are pursuing and they will learn more about themselves. Their confidence will also increase as they make progress.

💬 Short-Term Milestones questions

- Where on the journey do you want to be in twelve months' time?

- How would you know you are there? What will you see, hear and feel?

- What would be different for you and for others?

- What will be the same, if anything?

- What will the benefits be for you and for others?

SHORT-TERM MILESTONES IN PRACTICE

Yvonne worked for a government agency that had lots of international assignments and opportunities. Her husband worked for the same organisation and they had developed a picture of future success where they would work internationally for a few years before they started a family. That dream was a way off as Yvonne was still studying for her professional qualifications and, while she was excited by the idea, she was also nervous about it. She decided not to worry about the international assignment for now. Instead, her focus for the next year was to complete her professional qualifications and to spend time meeting and talking to as many people as possible who had lived and worked internationally to find out what the experience was like in different geographies and cultures.

 Tips for using the Short-Term Milestones tool

- Identify a relevant and meaningful timeframe – will it be three months? Six months? A year?

- Encourage them to be specific about the progress they want to make in that time.

- Explore observable signs that will indicate progress and success.

- Discuss benefits to themselves and others who may be affected.

#9 Setting Off tool: What actions will they take?

Taking the first step is usually the hardest part of the journey. Often, people are not sure about the best actions to take to reach their dream of future success. The temptation is to wait until the entire road map is available or the timing is perfect before they begin. That simply results in paralysis and procrastination.

The *Setting Off* tool is about encouraging the individual to commit to do-able actions that will help them make progress, however small. By identifying small, manageable steps to do immediately, energy can more easily be directed to implementation, which creates enthusiasm for further action. Small steps can result in large progress. There are several career development strategies they might consider:

1. Help them do their homework. There's no point in employees thinking about their own strengths and aspirations without thinking about how those could align with the goals and opportunities in the organisation. Encourage employees to research the organisation's vision, goals, opportunities and challenges. How could their picture of future success fit into the organisation? Does the role they want to develop already exist, at least in part, within the organisation? If not, how could it add most value to the organisation? How could it help the organisation achieve its vision, deliver its goals or respond to the key trends in the industry?

2. Help them identify the key people they need to influence. Career management is not just about what they know and want – it's also about who knows and wants them. Progressing towards their picture of future success requires them to identify the people they need to influence to shape their role. This could include you as their current manager who can approve a simple expansion of their current role, or it could be people and groups who need to believe in the possibilities of the new role they want to shape. What strategies can they use to raise their profile with these key decision-makers and demonstrate their credibility?

3. Encourage them to continually develop the knowledge, skills and resources they need. An organisation's processes are normally designed to achieve the needs of the organisation rather than an individual's career fulfilment. However, with the direction and energy of their future success, individuals can more assertively pursue formal and informal opportunities to take training, meet people and investigate opportunities that align with their career aspirations. Encourage them to keep up to date, read widely, make useful contacts and go to exhibitions and conferences.

4. Advise them to raise their profile in the organisation by making the best and most visible impact

they can. Help them learn the art of self-marketing and develop their 'personal brand' by making sure that they communicate three key messages: 1) what they do well, 2) how they make a difference and 3) the kinds of challenges and projects they'd like to take on so their career will develop.

5. Help them find mentor(s) and sponsor(s) to support them. To make progress in their career they will need the help, support and encouragement of others. Take some time to help them identify individuals who could assist in some way. Encourage them to find a way to inform these individuals of their aspirations and career goals and ask their advice on how best to make progress.

6. Encourage them to build their network and develop relationships. Even with the speed, ease of access and global reach of information, people still make decisions based on personal experience and relationships. We want to know, like and trust the people we work and partner with, so people will rely on their own experiences with a person and the references of those they trust. Their challenge is to take advantage of this situation by getting connected and expanding their network.

💬 Setting Off questions

- What steps will you take in the next three months to progress towards your short-term milestones?

- What are the first small steps towards that?

- What support do you need?

- Who can help you?

- What else needs to happen?

SETTING OFF IN PRACTICE

Let me share a story about myself. In January 2006, I decided to talk to someone about my own career. I developed a wonderful picture of future success that resulted in my husband and I deciding to relocate from London to Newcastle. He would get a job at one of the universities up there and I would continue as a Learning and Development professional. It was a huge decision. As with all careers, there were a few possible routes. The most obvious were that I could become self-employed and set up on my own, I could get a job with a company in Newcastle or I could continue with my current job, but relocate to Newcastle. My current employer was an insurance company based in the City of London with no presence whatsoever in Newcastle, but that would be the easiest route. I decided the small step I could take was to see if that was a possibility. I drafted a business case that outlined how I thought I could make it work and I took it to my manager. I fully expected him to say no and I would then have to hand in my resignation instead. To my surprise, he said yes. He didn't want to lose me, so they were happy to trial it for six months and see how it worked out. That small step of writing a business case made a massive difference.

Tips for using the Setting Off tool

- To identify actions, ask your employee to brainstorm a range of options and then discuss which would be the easiest. Which is most likely to succeed?

- Possible actions include research, talking to people, embarking on some form of training or professional development, raising their profile, finding mentors/sponsors, building their network and strategic relationships.

- Encourage them to commit to small steps they can take immediately.

#10 Progress Review tool: How are they getting on?

Development activity is only that – activity – until it is reflected on and learned from. The tenth and final tool is the *Progress Review* tool. It allows you to help the employee reflect on the journey, learn from the experience and continue to move forwards.

Career Conversations are typically not one-off conversations. They are iterative, emergent and ongoing. The *Progress Review* tool is designed to make sure that the conversation continues and that the employee continues to build on their progress with small steps. The *Progress Review* is deliberately worded. Quite often when we review progress, we take an approach where we say, 'You said you were going to take actions a, b and c. Have you completed them?' This review is kept open-ended, because you're not necessarily interested in a, b and c, you're interested in whether they've made progress. It may be that they decided against a, b and c, but d happened and that has really helped.

Organisations are always changing and life is always changing. Irrespective of whether somebody did what they said they were going to, they may still have made progress because an opportunity presented itself, or somebody came to them and had a conversation that they didn't expect, or presented them with a task that they suddenly discovered they loved. It's what I call 'the serendipity factor'. You want to gain feedback about progress that has resulted from these happy accidents as well as progress from deliberate actions that they've taken.

You may wish to recommend that employees keep a 'Success Journal' or 'Success Folder'. This is a place where they can keep a record of what they do well, the accolades that they've received and the results that they've been responsible for. It will be easier for them to review their progress and recall their successes and strengths when they have an accurate, up-to-date list to hand.

💬 Progress Review questions

- What progress have you made?

- What helped you make progress?

- Where are you on your journey now?

- What have you learned?

- What is your next small step?

PROGRESS REVIEW IN PRACTICE

When Helen came to the session, she immediately apologised for not completing the task she had set for herself in our previous session. Her focus was on developing her presentation skills as she knew they would be needed to progress her career as a research scientist. We had agreed that a good opportunity was to deliver a 'lunch and learn' session for her team and to get feedback from her team and her manager afterwards. Unfortunately, the session had been cancelled due to train strikes. I said, 'In spite of not being able to deliver the lunch and learn session, what progress have you made in developing your confidence with presenting to a group of people?' Helen explained that she had put a lot of effort into preparing for the session. She had read a book on presentation skills, she had watched a couple of TED talks and she had spoken to a colleague who was a good presenter and whom she admired. She had then applied what she had learned in preparing her session and she'd practised her presentation in private. We then went on to explore how she could build on that progress by practising her presentation in front of friends and rescheduling the lunch and learn.

Tips for using the Progress Review tool

- Keep a broad perspective. Don't limit the review to the agreed actions. Highlight *all* progress, no matter how small or where it came from.

- Explore what they did that contributed to progress, but also what others did and any happy coincidences that have taken place.

- Maintain momentum by agreeing next steps to build on progress.

That brings us to the end of our review of the tools in the Career Conversation Toolkit. I hope you have fun putting them into practice. In the next chapter, we're going to look at how you can use the tools in different ways.

PART 4
CAREER CONVERSATIONS IN PRACTICE

It's time to put the ideas in this book and the Career Conversation Toolkit into practice. In this section, we are going to spend some time sharing some good practice examples and thoughts on some common challenges and concerns managers might have when leading these types of conversations.

10
Bringing It All Together

In this chapter, we're going to look at the different ways you can use the *Career Conversation Toolkit*. You can use it on three different levels:

1. Focus on one question or one tool in a brief conversation or as homework.

2. Blend two to three different tools to address a specific question or challenge.

3. Apply all ten tools in an in-depth conversation or a series of conversations.

Using the Career Conversation Model and Toolkit

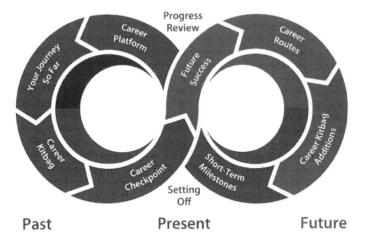

Past   Present   Future

I recommend that the exploration phase of your conversation loops around the Career Conversation Model in a figure of eight moving between the past, present and future. How deep you go and how many turns around the process you take will depend on the needs of the individual and the time available.

Exploration Phase	Career Conversation Tools
1. Start from where they are	Career Platform
	Progress Review
2. Learn from past experience	Your Journey So Far
	Career Kitbag
3. Open up future possibilities	Future Success
	Career Routes
	Career Kitbag Additions

4. Circle back to the present	*Career Checkpoint*
	Short-Term Milestones
	Setting Off

Phase 1: Start from where they are

People engage in career conversations when they need to set a new direction, plan for a change in role or feel dissatisfied with where they're at. Conversations are often triggered by 'crossroads decisions' they need to make soon. In this phase, you can use the *Career Platform* tool to establish where they are starting from and what they would like help with. If you have had previous conversations with them, you can use the *Progress Review* tool to find out how they are getting on and what they want to focus on.

Phase 2: Learn from past experience

You can then progress the conversation to move 'backwards' into the past. In this phase, you help employees identify what they already know about developing their career. The *Your Journey So Far* tool releases the energy and learning they gained from past experience. It helps reveal people's feelings about their careers so far. It helps them look back to understand where they've been and what they've learned along the way. It helps them to reflect on what they're good at, what's most important to them, what keeps them engaged and how they like to work.

This conversation can then progress to explore skills, achievements and learning using the *Career Kitbag* tool. Many people have forgotten the skills and abilities they have at their disposal, but are strongly aware of what's missing. With this tool you help them identify and focus on all the resources they have. You can also provide useful input. By recalling their achievements and all the success stories you've heard, you can give them genuine feedback about the positive skills, qualities, behaviours and attitudes that you've noticed.

Phase 3: Open up future possibilities

Career development is a journey, not a destination. In this phase, the conversation moves forwards into the future. You help employees discover the general direction they want to go in and the variety of routes and possibilities to get there. The *Future Success* tool helps unleash the person's imagination. It's important at this point to leave judgement behind and to help the person tune into their own intuition and feelings. It does not have to be worked out in detail, but should be a powerful representation of real aspirations.

The *Career Routes* tool starts to provide some real context to the future by helping employees explore the many ways to get to their destination. The choices available to them may include a change in role upwards or sideward, but the greatest opportunities often come from finding ways to help them develop in their current role. The *Career Kitbag Additions* tool grounds the situation further by analysing the specific development needed for different options.

Phase 4: Circle back to the present

For career conversations to be effective, they need to trigger action by the individual. In this phase, you help employees make the most of the journey by identifying small changes and actions that can make big differences. The *Career Checkpoint* tool links learning from the past with insights about the future to establish what is already in place and what progress has already been made.

The *Short-Term Milestones* tool helps translate long-term ambitions into an achievable goal and the *Setting Off* tool breaks that down into small steps and actions that can be taken immediately. By focusing on the immediate future, you can encourage them to commit to do-able actions which will help them make progress. By identifying small manageable steps to do immediately, they can direct their energy towards implementation. That creates enthusiasm for action. Small steps can result in large progress.

Getting prepared for success

If you know you are going to have a career conversation, some preparation will help you to shape and steer it. Think about the following:

- Prepare an opening so that you can quickly build rapport and develop trust.

- Review any previous notes or conversations you may have already had.

- Consider the individual's strengths and growth areas so you are ready with examples if required.

- Have a few powerful questions ready to start the process or move the conversation along.

- Remind yourself of the organisation's strategy and priorities so you can signpost growth areas or projects as development activities.

- Think about your own career journey and the lessons you have learned along the way.

Let's talk through some possible agendas for career conversations. There are a variety of them for you to try. Find what works best for you:

Agenda 1: Series of career conversations

Conversation 1	*Career Platform*
	Your Journey So Far
Conversation 2	*Future Success*
	Career Checkpoint
Conversation 3	*Career Kitbag*
	Career Routes
Conversation 4	*Career Kitbag Additions*
	Short-Term Milestones
	Setting Off
Conversation 5	*Progress Review*

Agenda 2: 60-minute conversation

5 minutes	Set up the conversation
10 minutes	*Career Platform*
10 minutes	*Future Success*
10 minutes	*Career Checkpoint*
5 minutes	*Short-Term Milestones*
10 minutes	Share information
5 minutes	*Setting Off*
5 minutes	Agree actions

Agenda 3: 20-minute conversation

1 minute	Set up the conversation
2 minutes	*Career Platform* – What would you like to be different?
5 minutes	*Future Success* – Suppose you could wave a magic wand and develop your career in exactly the way you'd like to. What would you be doing?
3 minutes	*Career Checkpoint* – On a scale of one to ten, where ten is your picture of Future Success, where are you today? Why are you that high and not lower? What's going well?
5 minutes	Share information
2 minutes	*Setting Off* – What steps will you take in the next x months to progress?
2 minutes	Agree actions

A case study

To help you see how this can work in practice, here is a case study one of my team members developed from a real career conversation at work:

Hettie was a young, enthusiastic HR officer. She was a highly intelligent graduate with great potential. She worked well with the internal teams across the business. She was good at establishing strong connections and sharing her insights and advice. She had a great way of communicating with the wider networks, too. Her communication style was open, friendly and authoritative. Her manager, Oona, wanted to make sure we made the most of her experience and talents within the organisation. She was doing well in HR, but Oona could see that a professional qualification would help underpin her instincts. When Oona suggested they could help her with the time or money to do the CIPD qualification, Hettie's face fell.

'Oh, I really don't want to be pigeonholed into HR. I love the project work, but really can't see myself in HR long-term.' This came as a complete surprise. Oona assumed that because she was a high achiever and she was enjoying her work, she would want to stay in HR through her career. It was time for a career conversation.

Career Conversation #1 – Learn from the past

In this first conversation, Oona used the *Your Journey So Far* tool to help them explore what motivates Hettie. She was able to identify when she was happiest and most satisfied at work, and they pulled out the attributes of a great work environment for her. Hettie shared that one of the key elements she loved in her current role was that she was included in news from the beginning. She knew that colleagues trusted her and often shared information with her before others. She liked being the central point of information for colleagues. She was particularly enjoying the rollout of communications about their reward project and even leading the all-staff meetings they had set up.

Career Conversation #2 – Dream about the future

In the second conversation, they focused on what the future might look like. Oona used a question posed in the *Future Success* tool. 'Suppose you could wave a magic wand and develop your career exactly the way you'd like to. What would that look and feel like?' Hettie shared a future where she would be meeting all stakeholders across the business and listening and engaging with them in focus groups. She liked to travel and visit centres across the UK. She would be contributing to dialogue with senior leaders on strategic developments. She would research, put in place and build the way we all work together developing the culture of the organisation. They talked about the skills and relationships that would help her achieve her aspirations. Then they started to think about a plan for developing them.

Career Conversation #3 – Take action

In the earlier conversations, they had talked about what motivated Hettie in the past and where she would like her ideal career path to take her. In the third conversation, they focused on identifying how she could get there. Hettie set herself a goal to be the HR Communications Lead over the next six months. She wanted to develop the all-staff team meetings and would lead the communication plan for the roll-out of the reward project they were working on. Oona suggested she spend some time with their external communications team, and she was going to set up a date to spend a day with them to shadow their work.

Over the next three months, Hettie and Oona revisited her plan and reviewed her progress. It was not always a smooth journey. Hettie needed to alter her plans to give her time to complete other projects, but she kept her eye on her end vision. Hettie progressed quickly and Oona was soon able to support Hettie by finding projects that would help her:

- Oona put her in charge of the all-staff meetings and the communication of the reward project outcomes.

- Hettie led the rollout of a staff engagement survey. She then managed the focus groups to discuss the results with the wider organisation across the UK. She reported back to the senior leadership group on the outcomes from staff.

- She worked with the comms team on the development of the employer brand and the development of the recruitment website.

In time, there was a vacancy for an Internal Communications Manager. This was a big jump for Hettie and there were many applicants with plenty of experience, but Hettie had developed a good relationship with the comms team. She was well known across the organisation for sharing news and she had proven experience in the digital development of the website. She was successful. She had taken her first steps to achieve her career ambitions and the organisation had retained her many talents.

11
Manager's Questions

Over the years I have heard several challenges that managers face and fear in relation to career conversations, but as Samuel Johnson wrote, 'Nothing will ever be attempted if all possible objections must first be overcome.'[22] In this chapter, I'll share some of the most common challenges and my thoughts on how best to address them.

How do I make time for career conversations?

I'm going to talk about one of the main challenges I hear from managers when I've asked how they have got on

---

22   S Johnson, *The History of Rasselas, Prince of Abissinia* (Publisher unknown, 1759)

with their career conversations. While there is always great progress from those who have tried conversations out, there are also some people who say they haven't had the chance. Managers are all busy. The question is, how do they find the time for career conversations?

The good news is that sustained behaviour change can be created through small steps. According to Dr BJ Fogg at Stanford University, behaviour and behaviour change is not as complicated as most people think. It's systematic. There are ways to understand behaviour that are straightforward and simple. In his book, *Tiny Habits: Why Starting Small Makes Lasting Change Easy*,[23] Fogg proposes that three elements must come together at the same time for a behaviour to occur. (1) The motivation for that behaviour, (2) The ability to perform the behaviour, and (3) A trigger. When someone doesn't behave the way you'd like, it's likely that at least one of those three elements is missing:

1. Motivation. You need to make your behaviour personal, positive and rewarding. Unless someone is willing to commit to a new goal, they are unlikely to make lasting changes in their behaviour. They won't take actions that will help them achieve that goal and turn it into a habit, so the first thing to focus on is motivation to change. What is the motivation for having those career conversations? I'm hoping that the earlier chapters will have motivated you to have

23   BJ Fogg, *Tiny Habits: Why Starting Small Makes Lasting Change Easy* (Virgin Books, 29 December 2020)

career conversations by showing you their benefits both personally and for your employees.

2. Ability. The biggest mistake managers make is to try to make huge changes. This is difficult, so they end up in a vicious loop. They feel demotivated because they are not making progress, so they stop trying and give up. To overcome this, the key is to start with small, doable 'baby steps'. Fogg explains that, 'in most situations behaviour change occurs only when the behaviour is easy to do.'[24] If you want to start having career conversations you need to start small, in fact, *very* small. Here are a few examples. Notice how 'micro' and easy they are:

- In a morning meeting, ask someone what's on the schedule that they're most looking forward to that day.

- At the coffee machine, say to someone, 'I've been doing a bit of a fun survey. If you could wave a magic wand and have the best afternoon at work ever, what would you be doing?'

- In an afternoon meeting, ask someone what they've enjoyed most about their work today and really listen to them.

- On your way out the door, ask someone, 'On a scale of one to ten, how was your day?' Even if

---

24 BJ Fogg, *Tiny Habits: Why Starting Small Makes Lasting Change Easy* (Virgin Books, 29 December 2020)

they give you a low score, laugh and say, 'Well at least it wasn't zero. What happened to save the day from being rock bottom?'

Bringing simple questions about careers into a casual and informal conversation might be the small step you need to get you started.

3. A trigger. For career conversations to become regular, they need to become a habit. They need to become routine rather than 'new'. Fogg recommends that you use an existing daily or weekly routine and link it to a simple and easy behaviour related to career conversations. If you regularly have one-to-one meetings with your employees, make it a habit to ask, 'What's been going well for you? What have you enjoyed about work recently? What has been your proudest achievement this week?' Just one conversation around careers at the start of the meeting can give both you and your employee some insight. Perhaps you have a daily routine like one of my old bosses. If he was in the office, he would always appear on our floor at some point in the afternoon. Maybe he thought, 'Whenever I get back from lunch, as long as I don't have a meeting scheduled, I'll walk about and just have a casual conversation with people about what's going on for them.' We loved the fact that he would turn up without an agenda and have a general conversation getting to know people.[25]

---

25 For further info on BJ Fogg's model see https://behaviormodel.org

What if my employee isn't interested in career development?

One comment I often hear is, 'My people are happy where they are. They don't care, they don't want to do anything different. How do I deal with that?'

There are a few points to think about here. One thought is, 'Do they need to care? Is it important that everybody aspires to do something different?' If they're happy and they're doing a good job and they are engaged and motivated, there is an argument that it's their choice. They may have other challenges outside of work that are stretching them and placing demands on them. Their priority might be to keep work as simple as possible so they have the energy they need for those life challenges.

You might think they're capable of a lot more and that they would enjoy the opportunity to develop. If that's the case, I recommend you help them see the benefits that would come from taking the development opportunities. Explore what's important to them and then explore how some new opportunities might help them get more of that. For example, they might get to attend a conference, work on a particular project or get more interesting work to do. They might get moved off a task or project they're bored of.

One specific scenario that often gets raised is employees who are heading into retirement. How do you manage career conversations with them? Again, I would explore what's important to them. Are they going to leave work having achieved everything that they want to achieve? Are they going to leave the organisation in the best place for people to follow them? Are they going to leave their role in such a way that somebody can carry on all the great work that they've started? How can they use their remaining time at work to prepare them for retirement?

My final thought on this relates to Pareto's principle. Also known as the 80/20 rule, the law of the vital few or the principle of factor sparsity, it states that for many events, roughly 80% of the effects come from 20% of the causes.[26] Applying the principle to career conversations, we can assume that 80% of positive responses will come from 20% of your people. That being the case, I recommend you start with the people who are most receptive and interested. Identify the 20% of your team with whom career conversations will make the biggest difference and start there. When other members of your team see their colleagues making progress, they may become more receptive.

---

26 MBN, 'What is the Pareto Principle? Definition and meaning' (Market Business News, no date), https://marketbusinessnews. com/financial-glossary/pareto-principle, accessed 23 March 2022

How do I create opportunities for development when budgets are tight?

It doesn't take a formal training programme for employees to develop the skills and experience needed to advance their careers. As a manager, you can integrate development into everyday activities to help improve employee satisfaction. At the same time, you'll improve the performance and productivity of your team. Here are four approaches that contribute to professional growth and development:

1. Job content and responsibilities. Development opportunities are not just found in training classes and seminars. You can have a significant impact on an employee's development through the responsibilities in an employee's current job. Employees will learn by doing – by working on real problems and dilemmas. It may be an entirely new job or a responsibility added to an existing job such as a short-term project. The key rule is challenge. It must be something that stretches people, pushes them out of their comfort zones and requires them to think and act differently.

2. Developmental relationships. One of the most powerful development options is learning through interaction with others. They can provide feedback and share information. They can coach and challenge. They can praise, support and reinforce. As their manager, you have an important role to play in helping them develop through coaching and career conversations. Mentoring is also a powerful tool for professional development and often has huge benefits for the mentor as well as the mentee.

3. Internal training and development. There are lots of opportunities for employees to help each other develop their knowledge and skills. Internal training and development bring a special plus. The examples used and the terminology reflect the culture and environment of your workplace in a way that external training does not. Employees can attend training sessions by colleagues or run a training session of their own. One of my clients put on a day-long conference with lunch at a nearby hotel. The conference sessions were almost all taught by internal staff on topics of interest to their internal audience. Employees loved it; they learned and enjoyed the day and gained a new respect for the knowledge and skills of their colleagues. Another client sponsored an employee book club during which employees discussed a current book and applied its concepts to the organisation.

4. External training and development. To help employees develop new skills and bring new ideas into your organisation, some external training is a must. Continuing education also enhances the knowledge, capabilities and experience of your employees. When employees attend external training, it's important to get the most value out of this. That requires the employees sharing the information with others to extend the value of the company's investment. Options include discussing, presenting or writing down what they got from a development opportunity. External training doesn't have to be hugely expensive. Online training, conferences and professional organisations provide affordable opportunities for employees to keep up with new developments in their field.

There are many ways you can help your employees grow and develop. The options are limited only by your imagination. As a final point, it's important that you make time for growth and development. Stretch assignments, new responsibilities, coaching, mentoring and training can be great learning opportunities, but you must be realistic. If you're adding new responsibilities and activities into someone's role, you need to figure out how to offload other tasks to make room for this or it becomes punishing, not developmental. By doing so, you can help create the job they want instead of watching them find it at another company.

What if they want something I can't give, like a promotion or a pay rise?

One of the biggest challenges that gets raised is along these lines. 'In our organisation plenty of people would like to advance their careers and move to a higher role, but low turnover and lack of budget and headcount means there are limited opportunities to promote someone.'

It comes down to negotiation. I recommend you adopt principled negotiation strategies as described in the book *Getting to Yes: Negotiating an agreement without giving in* by William Ury and Roger Fisher.[27] Ury and Fisher make the point that people routinely engage in position-based bargaining. Each side takes a position, argues for it and makes concessions to reach a compromise.

In career conversations, the positions taken are often irreconcilable. For example, an employee wants a promotion. The manager and organisation say promotion isn't possible because of low turnover, lack of budget and headcount. Those are the two positions. Promotion, no promotion. They are irreconcilable. Either the employee wins and they get promoted, or the organisation wins and the employee doesn't get promoted. In reality, it's always going to be the organisation that wins. The result is anger, resentment and a breakdown of the relationship. It's no wonder managers are nervous of having career conversations with employees!

'Principled negotiation' means changing the game by focusing on interests, rather than positions. A position often obscures what people really want when the aim of a career conversation is to satisfy their underlying interests. A position is something they have decided on. Their interests are what caused them to decide. Focusing on interests instead of positions makes it possible to generate options and come up with a solution.

---

27   W Ury & R Fisher, *Getting To Yes: Negotiating An Agreement Without Giving In* (Random House, Business, June 2012)

Behind irreconcilable positions lie many shared and compatible interests. For example, let's look at the interests an employee shares with their manager:

1. Both want stability. The manager doesn't want to lose the employee; the employee wants a permanent job.

2. Both want employee engagement. The manager wants a happy, productive employee; the employee wants to enjoy their job and experience at work.

3. Both want a good working relationship. The manager wants an employee who will do a good job; the employee wants a manager who is responsive to their needs.

4. Both want the employee to develop. The manager wants to maximise performance; the employee wants to improve their employability for the future.

They may also have interests that do not conflict, but simply differ:

1. The employee may want recognition that he's better than his peers. The manager will want to operate according to company policy.

2. The manager would like the security of knowing the employee is going to stay. The employee, knowing this is a good company, is indifferent to the idea of resigning.

Against these shared and divergent interests, the opposed interests of promotion or no promotion seem more manageable. The shared interests will likely result in enhancements to the role. Possibilities include new responsibilities and challenges, as well as further development opportunities. The divergent interests may be reconciled by giving the employee an important, company-wide project to lead. There may be verbal reassurance by the employee that he has no plans to leave.

You may be thinking, 'What if that's not enough? What if the employee is not happy with that?' Then that may be their choice. Unfortunately, we can't grant every employee's wish, whose wishes have to be balanced with the needs of the organisation. The best alternative might be to part companies. That isn't what anybody wants, but it's sometimes the only solution. I was once in that situation.

CASE STUDY: Antoinette

My first job after university was as Technical Brand Manager in P&G. It had started off as a people-focused role involved in consumer research but following a restructure, it became more focused on the science and formulation aspects of research. This didn't interest me, so I asked for a change in role.

I wanted a role in HR, but I also wanted to stay in Newcastle. My manager worked hard to understand the reasons for my request. I wanted to be more involved with people. I wanted responsibilities for training.

I wanted to be more involved in recruiting, developing and managing others. I had bought a flat in Newcastle. I had invested in my life there. My manager wanted to keep me, he wanted to develop me and he thought I had potential in the organisation.

Unfortunately, there wasn't an HR vacancy in Newcastle. We generated some options, which were to move to an HR role in Surrey or to move to a more people-related role in Newcastle. The Newcastle role available was more to do with professional and regulatory services than people development. Neither option ticked the boxes for me, so I decided the best alternative was to take voluntary redundancy. It wasn't the ideal solution, but I felt that they'd worked hard to do what they could for me and I recognised that they couldn't create an HR role in Newcastle just to keep me happy. Looking back at that scenario now, they had wanted to help me come to an answer that was right for me and I still hold P&G up as a great place to work.

How do I manage a mismatch between an employee's perception and my own?

This challenge comes up in a variety of different guises. One fear is that the employee sees themselves as having more potential than you feel they do. For example, 'What if they have an over-inflated sense of their own potential?', 'What if they've hit their plateau?' or, 'What if the career aspiration is beyond the person?'

My view is that while you can judge whether they are ready now, it's up to them to decide if they're going to be ready in the future. If an employee expresses an ambition, they are saying that they think they have the ability, they are motivated and want the opportunity. They need to understand that to get that opportunity, they need to show that they are committed to the organisation. They need to embrace the challenges and responsibilities involved and they need to prove that they can do a good job.

Let's make a parallel with personal fitness. If I say I'm going to run the London Marathon next April, you might look me up and down and say, 'Really? You don't look like a runner. I don't think you're up to running a marathon.' Who are you to judge? If I really wanted to do it and was committed to it, it would be up to me to do what was necessary. I would have to sign up to the race and pay my entry fee. I would need to get the training shoes and buy the kit. I'd need to put together a training plan, get up at six in the morning, and put the training in whatever the weather. I would be successful or not on my own merits, plus a certain amount of opportunity. The training might return dividends and I might make great progress. On the other hand, I might get injured, or I might hate every minute and decide it's not for me. Whatever the outcome, I would have decided on my ambition and taken the steps needed to work towards it.

Let's bring this back to career conversations. If an employee says, 'I have this ambition, I'm motivated to make it a reality and I believe that I can develop the skills needed,' then who are we to judge? There needs to be a conversation about what the employee needs to do to show that they are committed to the organisation. They need to prove they are willing to take on everything involved. If they don't have the ability to take it on immediately, there needs to be a conversation about the development and support they need. If you give that person opportunities and support and they don't respond to it, then you can decide this isn't the right path for that individual. Hopefully though, they will have determined that for themselves through their own experience.

What if they expect me to have all the answers?

A common question I get asked is, 'How do I provide insight without direction? I want to help. I know they're coming to me for advice. I don't have all the answers.' You don't need to. While managers and mentors can share valuable experience and ideas, they don't need to have all the answers. They just need to have the questions to stimulate critical thought. How do you do this? I recommend three guiding principles when it comes to stimulating thought and generating ideas:

1. Generate as many insights and ideas as possible: Do so without judgement or evaluation. When it comes to solving a problem or making progress in a career,

there are many more options than are immediately obvious. Some of the options may seem unachievable or unappealing, but include them anyway. I think of it as creating a whole smorgasbord of ideas and opportunities. It helps to explore ideas and experiences from a range of sources. The first source is the employee reflecting on their own knowledge and experience. You can use questions like:

- What was the best you ever did (at this thing)?

- What went well then?

- When have you made great progress in your career before?

- What did you do that helped?

- When you've made career decisions before, what helped you reach the right answer?

The second source is the knowledge and experience of others. You can use questions like:

- Who else do you know who's made this career move?

- What strategies did they use?

The third source is your own knowledge and experience. You have useful experience and wisdom to offer and employees want to hear it, but I urge you to take care in how and when you do it (as explained in Chapter 9).

2. Start with insights from the employee first: If employees are going to take ownership for their career development, they need to act on the insights. They are much more likely to do that if they came up with them in the first place. It's better to explore the employees' own thoughts, experience and know-how first. If you don't do this, in the context of what he or she wants, they may well greet your ideas with a response like, 'I've tried that. It didn't work,' or, 'That wouldn't work,' or, 'I haven't got time for that.' Think about it. Have you ever tried to lose weight? Like most people, I have. Many times! Now, there is no shortage of insights into how to lose weight. Ask 100 different people and you'll hear 100 different experiences. Insights range from low-carb eating to slimming clubs to fasting and running marathons. Every single idea and option are possibilities. Yet, there are only a handful of them that I would consider trying. Let's say I go to my mentor to talk it through and he starts sharing his experience of losing 20kg through meal replacements. I'm likely to do one of two things. I'm either going to sign up for meal replacements thinking, 'I'd better try this because my mentor says this is the answer,' or I'm going to stop listening and think, 'It's all right for him, but that would never work for me.' Either way, I won't be energised and empowered to take action and lose weight. Imagine a different scenario.

This time when I go to my mentor, he says, 'I'm happy to share my experience of losing 20kg. Before we do that, let's discuss the thoughts you've had. You mentioned you've lost weight in the past. What helped then?' I would then rattle off insights from my own experience. (If you're interested, they include calorie counting, running, wedding (a goal) and divorce (stress!). Other behaviours that helped were low-carb, giving up alcohol and giving up chocolate.) My mentor listens and asks questions to explore the different experiences. Then he goes on to ask, 'What about friends and family? Do you know anyone else that's lost weight?' In response, I generate a whole new set of ideas based on what I know of others (slimming clubs, 5:2, Atkins, etc) Finally, my mentor says, 'I did something different. Let me share my experience.' He tells me about how he lost four stone using meal replacements supported by counselling. That brings me to my third principle.

3. Share your own insights in such a way that they can be rejected: When someone has chosen to talk to you about their career or sees you as a mentor, they have awarded you a degree of authority and respect. They are likely to see your insights as 'expert advice' even if you don't intend them that way. To avoid that, you need to make sure they can reject them if they don't suit them.

I've used the example of weight loss because it's universal, but the same principles apply to career challenges and business problems.

Conclusion

The inspiration for this book was all the managers we have trained who have found the Career Conversation Model and Toolkit so valuable in building their confidence to have career conversations with their employees.

As we have explored the concept of career conversations and the tools in the Career Conversation Toolkit, I hope the book has removed some of the fear from career conversations and reminded you that you already have many of the skills you need to empower your employees and help them take ownership of their career development.

In Part 1, I introduced you to the new rules of career growth. We looked at how the world of work has changed (and is still changing) and how we need to talk about career development differently in response. We learned the different responsibilities for career management in an organisation and the importance of a three-way partnership between employees, managers and the organisation. We then looked at why career conversations are important and the costly consequences if they don't take place, as well as the valuable benefits when they do.

In Part 2, we identified the characteristics of effective career conversations, including the importance of a growth mindset and separating career conversations from performance reviews. Then we explored the power of different questions to develop self-awareness. We went on to look at the value of using solution-focused questions to empower employees to take ownership of their career development. I then introduced you to the Career Conversation Model and Toolkit which have been designed to provide you with a set of powerful solution-focused questions and a framework for career conversations.

In Part 3, we worked through the different tools in the Career Conversation Toolkit:

1. **Career Platform:** Helps an employee determine what they want to change in their career and motivates them to take action.

2. **Your Journey So Far:** Allows employees to reflect on what they're good at, what's most important to them and how they like to work.

3. **Career Kitbag:** Helps employees identify all the resources they have that will help them make progress. Skills include technical skills, soft skills and career development skills.

4. **Future Success:** Helps employees articulate their ambitions by describing what success will look like.

5. **Career Routes:** Helps employees identify the options available to them in their current role and/or in new roles.

6. **Career Kitbag Additions:** Helps employees analyse the skills, experiences, information and relationships that they need to develop to progress toward their future success.

7. **Career Checkpoint:** Connects employees' ambition with reality to identify how their current situation is satisfying their aspirations and the progress they have made.

8. **Short-Term Milestones:** Helps employees focus on an achievable goal in the not-too-distant future.

9. **Setting Off:** Encourages employees to commit to doable actions that will help them make progress, however small.

10. **Progress Review:** Helps employees learn from the experience.

In each case, we looked at what each tool does, relevant questions, an example of how the tool works in practice and some tips for when you use it yourself.

In Part 4, we brought it all together by looking at different ways you can use the Career Conversation Model and Toolkit. We brought that to life with a case study of how they were used across a series of three conversations. Finally, we looked at ways to answer the questions that other managers have raised about career conversations that you may also be wondering about.

I hope you've enjoyed the read and that I've opened your eyes to the power of career conversations to empower your people and help them realise their potential and fulfil their ambitions. I hope that you, too, are feeling empowered to have those conversations with skill and confidence. As we have discussed in the book, small steps can make a big difference, so start small. Start with the people who will be most receptive. Start with just one question or one tool and see the positive impact it has.

If you would like to attend an in-person event, you can learn more about our one-day Confident Career Conversations Workshop at www.antoinetteoglethorpe.com/services/career-conversations/confident-career-conversations-workshop.

If you prefer self-study in your own time and at your own pace, details of our fully self-directed Confident Career Conversations Online programme can be found at https://antoinetteoglethorpe.teachable. com/p/confident-career-conversations-online.

You can purchase a physical or digital copy of the *Confident Career Conversations* toolkit at www. antoinetteoglethorpe.com/resources/career-conversation-toolkit and if you've not done so already, don't forget to check out the other free resources we have available to help you at www.antoinetteoglethorpe. com/resources.

Good luck! Enjoy your conversations and let me know how you get on. You can reach me by email on antoinette@antoinetteoglethorpe.com.

Acknowledgements

While I have written this book in the first person, it is very much the product of more than one individual. The collective includes many wonderful people who I have had the privilege to learn from and work with.

I'd like to thank Team AO, all of whom are incredibly talented and amazingly supportive. In particular, I'd like to thank Gwen Tredinnick, who helps us secure the most amazing clients to work with; Jenny O'Brien for keeping us all organised so we provide fantastic service to our clients and Clare Roberts for leading our facilitators so our clients get an amazing experience.

I'd like to thank the many clients I have worked with individually and in groups who have inspired the stories in this book. I've learned so much and grown so much as a result, I often think I have the best job in the world.

I'd like to thank all the mentors I have had during my career who have shared their hard-won experiences and insights so generously. In particular, I'd like to thank Mark McKergow, whose work with Solutions Focus principles continues to inspire and sits at the heart of the approach to career conversations described in this book. I'd also like to thank David Clutterbuck, who has inspired me through his many books and articles about mentoring, coaching and leader development. It is a real honour that he has written the foreword for this book.

I am also hugely grateful to Rob Nathan, who trained me as a career coach all those years ago and empowered me to follow my passion of bringing career conversations into the workplace.

I owe a massive debt of gratitude to all the colleagues, coaches and students I have worked alongside and learned so much from over the years.

Thank you to Lucy McCarraher, Joe Gregory and the team at Rethink Press, without whom this book would never have existed. Thanks also to all the test readers of the book who gave me such invaluable feedback – Mike Elliston, Dave Oglethorpe, Clare Roberts, Beate Giffo-Schmitt, Melanie Pearl and Kathryn Walker.

And finally, a huge thanks to my family. My wonderful husband Dave and the Oglethorpe family who encourage me and support me in everything I do. And my sister, Fiona, who has believed in me from the day I was born and is there with me every step of the way, even when she lives thousands of miles away.

The Author

Antoinette Oglethorpe is a multi-award-winning consultant, coach, speaker and author. Following a successful international career as a Learning and Organisational Development Director for Accenture, Avanade and FTSE 500 companies, she is highly experienced in supporting people with their professional development. She now brings that understanding to coaching, mentoring and leadership development.

She is the founder of her eponymous company, Antoinette Oglethorpe Ltd, a training and coaching company that specialises in career management and mentoring.

Unlike traditional career support which focuses on promotions and pay rises, Antoinette and her team, Team AO, are passionate about enjoyability and employability. Their mission is to help people realise their potential and fulfil their ambitions so that organisations benefit from the increased productivity that results when people are happier at work.

Antoinette has created unique models, tools and templates to help managers and employees have meaningful conversations about progression and development. Her Confident Career Conversations Workshop is a one-day workshop delivered in-person or online and designed to provide managers, mentors, coaches and HR professionals with the practical skills and tools to have meaningful career conversations. The approaches taught are now being used by the World Health Organization, the NHS and government departments, among others.

Antoinette is a Chartered Fellow of the CIPD and a Fellow of the Institute of Leadership and Management. She is also a Fellow of the Association for Coaching.

Antoinette frequently provides free resources to HR practitioners via her website. She speaks at events across the globe on subjects like the impact of mentoring and the importance of career conversations to engage, keep and develop leaders, among other talent development topics.

Antoinette is also the author of the book *Grow Your Geeks: A Handbook for Developing Leaders in High-Tech Organisations,* which achieved Number 1 Bestseller status on Amazon in the Leadership and Management category.

You can find Antoinette and Team AO at:

- www.antoinetteoglethorpe.com
- www.facebook.com/AntoinetteOglethorpe
- www.linkedin.com/in/antoinetteoglethorpe
- https://twitter.com/antoinetteog
- www.instagram.com/antoinetteog

Printed in Great Britain
by Amazon